"An accessible, well-researched and capti
ogy informs human behaviour. Methodo
students to understand a range of biological measures and, crucially, their significance. This thoughtful, focused and quirky approach, making clever use of diagrams and vivid examples, will help students navigate this vast area confidently and with understanding."

Lynn Wright, C.Psychol, AFBPsS *and* **Scott Hardie C.Psychol, AFBPsS**, *Faculty of Applied and Social Sciences, Abertay University, Scotland, UK*

"In this book, Karlsson and Ocklenburg present a succinct yet incredibly broad and accessible guided tour of psychobiology. The slim volume covers historical people and perspectives that were key to establishing the field, through to modern societal factors impacting behavioural and brain function and methods for measurement. This book is an essential resource for all psychology students and an enticing read for anyone with a passing interest in psychobiology."

Gillian S. Forrester, *Professor of Comparative Cognition and Academic Lead for Public Engagement, University of Sussex, England, UK*

"By distilling a wide-ranging literature into crisp explanations with clear, real-world relevance, this book makes a complex domain highly accessible. It is an indispensable guide to neurodiversity, stress biology, climate psychobiology, and intelligence – either biological and artificial – delivered with clarity and insight."

Silvia Paracchini, PhD, FRSB, FRSE, *Professor of Neurogenetics and Genomics, University of St Andrews, Scotland, UK, and Professor of Neurodevelopment Genomics, University of Bonn, Germany*

"This book offers an elegant and accessible roadmap to psychobiology, combining foundational neuroscience, core theories, and contemporary applications – such as climate psychobiology and artificial intelligence integration in psychobiology – in a way that is both rigorous and highly readable. It is ideally suited for undergraduate students looking for a first, inspiring encounter with the biological bases of behaviour."

Marietta Papadatou-Pastou, DPhil, *Associate Professor of Neuropsychology, National and Kapodistrian University of Athens, Greece*

Key Topics in Psychobiology

Key Topics in Psychobiology is a compelling introduction to the science of psychobiology, offering a thorough exploration of its historical foundations, theoretical principles, research methods, societal impacts, and emerging areas of inquiry. Written by expert researchers, this text provides readers with a clear framework for understanding the biological underpinnings of human behaviour.

This book begins by establishing the importance of psychobiology in explaining psychological functions and processes. It then examines key theoretical principles that have shaped the field, providing insights into the foundational ideas driving research. A detailed overview of psychobiological methods follows, including studies on brain lesions, neuroimaging techniques, and measures of electrical and magnetic activity in the brain, showcasing the tools that uncover the biological basis of behaviour. The societal impacts of psychobiological research are explored, with discussions on its contributions to address challenges such as dementia and addiction. Finally, this book concludes with a forward-looking perspective on emerging areas, including climate psychobiology and the intersection of human and artificial intelligence, highlighting the exciting directions the field is set to take.

Both informative and engaging, *Key Topics in Psychobiology*, is an invaluable resource for undergraduate and postgraduate students in psychology and related disciplines.

Emma M. Karlsson is a postdoctoral researcher at Ghent University, Belgium, whose work focuses on the structure and function of the brain.

Sebastian Ocklenburg is Professor of Research Methods at MSH Medical School Hamburg, Germany, where he conducts research on several topics within psychobiology.

BPS Key Topics in Psychology

British Psychological Society

Routledge, in partnership with the British Psychological Society (BPS), is pleased to present *BPS Key Topics in Psychology*, a series of short introductory books that focus on a specific field within psychology. Each book is broken down into bitesize chunks to provide a helpful overview of core psychology topics, made clear by a five-part structure: foundations, theories, methodologies, impacts, and emerging areas. Written by active and experienced authors, these essential books encourage students to approach fundamental concepts with confidence and critical thinking.

Books may incorporate student-friendly pedagogies, including tools such as: feature boxes; key terms and definitions; and links to further reading online. Concise yet comprehensive, these books offer a simple and accessible overview of core psychology topics for students looking for a summary of key concepts in the topic, or those new to the area.

Key Topics in Memory
Richard J. Allen and Charity Brown

Key Topics in Parenting and Family Psychology
Alina Morawska & Amy E. Mitchell

Key Topics in Identity Development
Theo A. Klimstra

Key Topics in Psychobiology
Emma M. Karlsson and Sebastian Ocklenburg

For more information about this series, please visit: www.routledge.com/BPS-Key-Topics-in-Psychology/book-series/BPSKTP

Key Topics in Psychobiology

Emma M. Karlsson and
Sebastian Ocklenburg

Routledge
Taylor & Francis Group
LONDON AND NEW YORK

Designed cover image: Getty Images / DrAfter123

First published 2027
by Routledge
4 Park Square, Milton Park, Abingdon, Oxon OX14 4RN

and by Routledge
605 Third Avenue, New York, NY 10158

Routledge is an imprint of the Taylor & Francis Group, an informa business

British Library Cataloguing-in-Publication Data
A catalogue record for this book is available from the British Library

ISBN: 9781032945859 (hbk)
ISBN: 9781032933344 (pbk)
ISBN: 9781003571537 (ebk)

DOI: 10.4324/9781003571537

Typeset in Galliard
by codeMantra

Access the Support Material: www.routledge.com/9781032933344

In loving memory of Anna and Smilla.

Contents

About the authors

Originally from Sweden, **Emma M. Karlsson** completed her PhD at Bangor University amid the beautiful landscapes of North Wales. She is a postdoctoral researcher at Ghent University, where she studies the function and structure of the brain. Her research explores how the two hemispheres of the brain process information, with a particular interest in handedness. Emma has received a Women in Neuroscience Award from the American Psychological Association and currently serves as co-president of the Ghent University Postdoctoral Community Steering Committee.

Born in Germany, **Sebastian Ocklenburg** is Professor of Research Methods at MSH Medical School Hamburg, where he conducts research on several topics within psychobiology. These include hemispheric asymmetries, social neuroscience, and how the climate crisis affects the brain. He has authored over 180 international peer-reviewed publications and six books on psychobiology and is an active science blogger who tries to present psychobiological research in an interesting and fun way for the general public.

Preface

There is no psychology without biology, and there is no "you" without a brain. Without the brain, there would be no first kisses in the rain, no poetry, no art, no democracy, no weddings, and none of the myriad other things that make life so unique and extraordinary. Every memory, every fear, and every dream you have ever had depend on this intricate living tissue. As such, it is essential for every psychologist to understand the basics of how the brain works and how research methods focused on biological processes have informed psychological understanding. We hope that this book gives the reader a fascinating first insight into the world of psychobiological research. We certainly had fun writing it.

Gent & Hamburg, 2026
Emma M. Karlsson & Sebastian Ocklenburg

Acknowledgements

We would like to thank Jette Borawski for creating the beautiful artwork in this book. We also would like to thank Gillian Forrester, Lynn Wright, Marietta Papadatou-Pastou, Scott Hardie, and Silvia Paracchini for reading the preliminary version of this book and providing endorsements as well as Mathias Kauff for further feedback.

Section 1

Key foundations

This section aims to introduce the foundations of psychobiology, describing why it is so fundamental for understanding psychological function in health and disease. It will then give an overview of basic brain anatomy, signal generation, and information transfer in the nervous system.

At the end of section one, you will:

- Know what psychobiology is and how it relates to other disciplines within psychology
- Understand basic neuroanatomy
- Know how neuronal signals are generated in neurons and how they are transferred over axons and synapses
- Understand the roles of different types of neurotransmitters and hormones that are active in the nervous system

DOI: 10.4324/9781003571537-1

Chapter 1

From brain to behaviour

An introduction to psychobiology

Introduction

Few topics spark curiosity quite like the intricate nature of human behaviour. Perhaps you have always wondered how serial killers think, or how people can commit vicious crimes? How do athletes manage to stay calm under pressure? Or perhaps why public speaking is anxiety-induced hellscapes for some, when others find it exhilarating? Regardless of the aspect of human behaviour that piques your curiosity, we can trace parts of its origin back to one organ: the brain. Psychological experiences are inseparable from biology, as the way we think, feel, and act are all the result of complicated processes that happen in the brain. Therefore, to understand any kind of behaviour, we need to consider the functioning of the brain as it navigates the social and physical world.

What is psychobiology?

Psychology is the scientific study of the mind and behaviour. **Psychobiology**, also known as biopsychology or biological psychology, is a branch of psychology focused on understanding the biological mechanisms underlying behaviour. It is a very broad field, and psychobiologists explore how several psychological factors, such as mental processes, mood, or appraisal, interact with biological events such as brain function changes, genetics, or stress responses to influence psychological processes and behaviour. This is performed by applying **the scientific method**, a structured, evidence-

Psychobiology: The branch of psychology focused on understanding the biological mechanisms underlying behaviour. Also known as biopsychology or biological psychology.

DOI: 10.4324/9781003571537-2

The scientific method: A structured evidence-based approach to acquire knowledge.

Neuroscience: The multidisciplinary scientific study of the nervous system.

The mind-body problem: Debate concerning the relationship between the mind and the body.

based approach to acquire knowledge. Psychobiologists' research interests span a wide range of domains, from what happens in the brain when we think, to the biology underlying mental health disorders such as eating disorders, to the plasticity of the nervous system, and even what happens in the brain when we hug other people! Given the wide range of topics studied in psychobiology, it is not surprising that both researchers and their methods come from diverse backgrounds, including biology, medicine, physiology, and chemistry. This interdisciplinary approach to behaviour is part of the broader field of **neuroscience**, the multidisciplinary scientific study of the nervous system, with psychobiology representing one of its key components.

Historical roots of psychobiology

Psychobiology is a relatively new scientific discipline, but its roots trace back to early philosophers, where thinkers debated the origins of the mind. Some of the earliest recorded debates date back to the works of Greek philosophers, including Aristotle (4th century Before Common Era [BCE]), who argued that the chest or heart was the seat of thought and behaviour. However, other Greek writers assigned a much more important role to the brain, including Hippocrates (5th–4th century BCE) and Galen (2nd century CE). Ibn Sina (also known as Avicenna, 980–1037 CE) was a Persian physician and one of the first to relate physiology and psychology. He, amongst other things, developed a system in which he related pulse rate to inner feelings in the treatment of illnesses related to emotions.

Andreas Vesalius (1514–1564), a Belgian physician, is often regarded as the founder of anatomy. He revolutionised the study of biology and medicine with his detailed description of the anatomy of the human body. Around the same time, philosophers debated **the mind-body problem** (the debate of understanding the relationship between the mind and the body). French philosopher René Descartes (1596–1650) argued for dualism, the idea that mind and body are separate from one another. However, he later recognised that mind and body had to interact in some way and suggested that this might happen through the pineal gland, as it was unique in the sense that it was non-paired (as you will see in Chapter 2, many structures in the brain come in pairs in each of the two sides of the brain).

Psychology was founded as a scientific discipline in Germany in 1879 by Wilhelm Wundt (1832–1920). At that time, psychology relied primarily on introspection to study conscious experience (e.g., sensations and feelings), and Wundt aimed to transform it into a more empirically rigorous science. Wundt instead started using experimental methods, such as reaction time studies, to investigate behaviour. Shortly after, William James (1890) argued that the scientific study of psychology should be grounded in an understanding of biology by framing mental processes as biological functions. Although there is no exact date that psychobiology was born, the earliest recorded works that referenced the terminology were by Argentine psychiatrist José Ingenieros (1877–1925) in 1910 and in 1914 by American psychologist Knight Dunlap (1875–1949). Dunlap was also the first editor-in-chief of the journal *Psychobiology*, which further recognised the discipline as its own scientific field (Dewsbury, 1991).

Noteworthy figures in psychobiological research

Throughout this book, you will read about many prolific researchers, physicians, and clinicians who, together with their teams, have contributed significantly to the study of psychobiology. In addition, we have highlighted some of the people who have made significant contributions to the study of the brain and behaviour.

Santiago Ramón y Cajal (1852–1934)

Santiago Ramón y Cajal was a Spanish histologist and neuroscientist, and is often referred to as the father of modern neuroscience for his crucial theoretical advances in the field. He was awarded the Nobel Prize in Physiology or Medicine in 1906 together with Camillo Golgi in recognition of his work on the structure of the nervous system. He, for example, discovered that neurons are individual units and communicate through a specialised junction or structure called a synapse (see Chapter 3).

Cécile Vogt (1875–1962)

Cécile Vogt was a French neuropathologist who made a significant contribution to our understanding of the structure of the brain, together with her husband Oskar Vogt. She was one of the first women to attend medical school in France and received her doctorate in medicine in 1900. Together with a team of female technicians, she traced connections in the brain and archived over thousands of brain sections that would form one of the most extensive collections in the world, now housed in the Cécile and Oskar Vogt Brain Research Collection in Düsseldorf, Germany.

Rita Levi-Montalcini (1909–2012)

Rita Levi-Montalcini was an Italian neurobiologist. She studied medicine and later started studies in neurology and psychology but was banned from pursuing a career in science because of anti-Jewish laws. Instead, she continued her research in a laboratory she built in her own bedroom. Here, she continued to study neurons. Rita Levi-Montalcini contributed significantly to our knowledge of cell division and was awarded the Nobel Prize in Physiology or Medicine in 1986, together with biochemist Stanley Cohen, for their discoveries of nerve growth factors, which are vital proteins that promote the survival and growth of specific neurons.

Roger Wolcott Sperry (1913–1994)

Roger Wolcott Sperry was an American psychobiologist who is most known for his work with "split-brain" patients, which significantly advanced our knowledge of the specialisation of the two sides of the brain and the treatment of epilepsy. He received the Nobel Prize in Physiology or Medicine in 1981 for his discoveries concerning the functional specialisation of the two sides of the brain.

Patricia Goldman-Rakic (1937–2003)

Patricia Goldman-Rakic was an American neurobiologist and neuroscientist. Her pioneering work included discoveries about an area in the front of the brain called the prefrontal cortex and the biological basis of working memory. She was elected to the National Academy of Sciences in 1990 and was awarded several prizes for her outstanding contributions to our understanding of the brain.

Conclusion

Psychobiology is a rather new scientific discipline concerned with the scientific study of the relationship between biological processes, such as brain function, hormones, and genetics, and behaviour. Its origins lie in the intersection of biology and psychology, and questions relevant to the field can be traced back to early Greek philosophers. Psychobiology is a wide field of study, and scientists with very diverse backgrounds have contributed to the modern knowledge that we have of the brain and behaviour.

Further reading

Additional academic source: Catani, M., & Sandrone, S. (2015). *Brain Renaissance: From Vesalius to Modern Neuroscience*. Oxford University Press. https://doi.org/10.1093/med/9780199383832.001.0001

Related documentary: *My Love Affair with the Brain: The Life and Science of Dr. Marian Diamond* (2016). A documentary profile of a brilliant neuroscientist.

Relevant web resource: https://www.bps.org.uk/, the website of the British Psychological Society (BPS), the representative body for psychology and psychologists in the UK.

Relevant web resource: https://www.storiesofwin.org/, the website of Stories of Women in Neuroscience, a collection of profiles showcasing Women in Neuroscience.

References

Dewsbury, D. A. (1991). Psychobiology. *American Psychologist, 46*(3), 198–205. https://doi.org/10.1037/0003-066X.46.3.198

James, W. (1890). *The Principles of Psychology*. Henry Holt and Co.

Chapter 2

Two halves, one brain

A quick introduction to the neuroanatomy of the nervous system

Introduction

At first glance, the human brain may look like a humongous brownish-grey mass that has, as British computer science pioneer Alan Turing once famously remarked, the "consistency of cold porridge". This impression is false, as the brain is quite an intricate structure. Neuroanatomy is the study of the nervous system's structure and organisation. While there is remarkable variability in the size and shape of human brains, they all feature the same anatomical blueprint and have specific anatomical landmarks that can be used as reference points. The **neuron**, together with supporting cells, is the fundamental building block of the nervous system (Figure 2.1). The neuron is a specialised cell that acts as a messenger in the nervous system. A neuron has three main parts: the soma (cell body) with the nucleus inside, the tree-like dendrites that branch out to receive signals from other neurons, and the axon, a long extension that carries received signals away from the cell body to other neurons. More information about neurons and neuronal signalling is provided in Chapter 3.

> **Neuron**: A fundamental building block in the CNS that acts as an information messenger.

The nervous system

The nervous system is the body's internal information processing system. It receives information about the environment from sensory organs like the eyes and also processes information from internal receptors throughout the body. It also activates muscles, so that we can interact with our environment. The complexity of the nervous system is so remarkable that it is hard to grasp. The total length of myelinated nerve fibres in the body

DOI: 10.4324/9781003571537-3

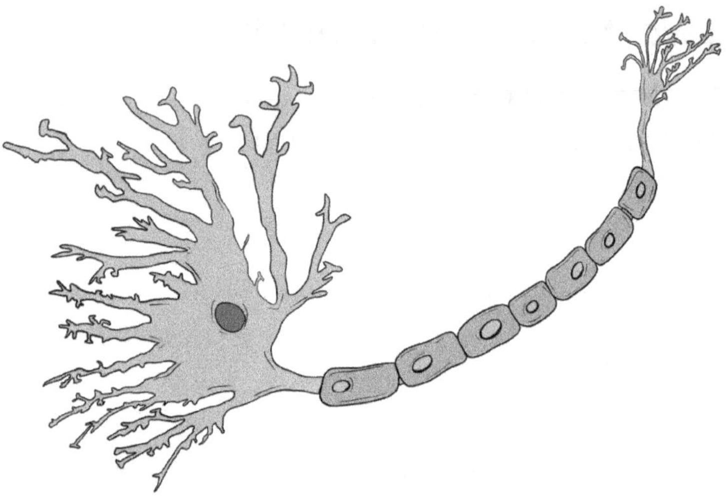

Figure 2.1 A figure of a neuron showing its three main parts: the dendrites, the soma (cell body), and the axon. The soma contains the nucleus (the dark middle structure), while the dendrites branch out from the soma to receive signals from other neurons. Extending from the soma is the axon, a long projection that carries signals to other neurons. The axon is wrapped in a myelin sheath, depicted as an additional insulating layer in brown, and ends in the axon terminals, which connect with other neurons.

has been estimated to be around 150,000–180,000 kilometres (Pakkenberg et al., 2003). With the distance around the Earth being around 40,075 kilometres, the nerve fibres of a single person could wrap around the whole planet several times.

The brain, along with the spinal cord, forms the central nervous system (CNS), one of the two main divisions of the nervous system. The other division is the peripheral nervous system (PNS), which includes nerves and neurons outside the brain and spinal cord. Although psychobiology mainly focuses on the CNS to explore brain–behaviour relationships, the PNS interacts with the CNS to transmit messages throughout the body, as you will read in subsequent chapters. The CNS processes this information to determine appropriate responses, then sends commands back to the body via the PNS.

The central nervous system

The CNS is made up of the brain and spinal cord and serves as your body's main "processing centre". The **spinal cord** is a long extension

Spinal cord: A long extension of nerves that runs from the base of the brain to the lower back. This is the main route for information entering and leaving the nervous system.

Nerves: Groups or bundles of axons that are wrapped tightly together to quickly and efficiently transfer information.

Grey matter: Tissue that primarily consists of cell bodies and dendrites, which process information.

White matter: Tissue that primarily consists of the myelinated axons that carry information.

Cerebrospinal fluid (CSF): A clear liquid found in the central nervous system. Has several vital functions, such as support, homeostasis, supplying nutrients, and removing waste.

Cerebral ventricles: Hollow, interconnected spaces within the brain. Contains cerebrospinal fluid.

of **nerves** (groups of axons, individual nerve fibres that are wrapped tightly together) that runs from the base of the brain down the spine to the lower back. It is the main route for information entering and leaving the nervous system, while the brain acts as the main processing hub of all information. The CNS is mostly made up of grey matter and white matter. **Grey matter** consists mainly of neuronal cell bodies that process information, and **white matter** consists primarily of the axons that connect and transfer information between different areas.

The CNS also contains a clear liquid that surrounds the brain and spinal cord, called **cerebrospinal fluid** (CSF). This fluid is mainly produced in the **cerebral ventricles**, hollow interconnected spaces within the brain. CSF has several vital functions: it provides cushioning and support for the brain, especially during sudden head movements (essentially, it acts like a shock absorption pad); it regulates the brain's temperature and pressure (homeostasis), supplies the CNS with essential nutrients, and assists in removing waste products from the brain.

The peripheral nervous system

The PNS consists of nerves that extend throughout the body and connect to the CNS. The PNS can be divided into two parts: the autonomic and somatic nervous systems. The **somatic nervous system** interacts with the outside world: it processes sensory information such as the things you touch, smell, taste, and hear, and it also sends signals to muscles to generate voluntary movements. The somatic nervous system also produces involuntary, or automatic, movements, like the reflex that draws your hand away when you accidentally put it on a hot stove. Nerves that carry information from the CNS to the body are called **efferent nerves**, and those that carry information from the body into the CNS are called **afferent nerves.** The major nerves that make up the somatic nervous system are the **cranial nerves** (nerves connected directly to the brain) and the **spinal nerves** (nerves connected directly to the spinal cord).

> **Somatic nervous system:** Part of the PNS. Carries sensory information to the CNS and produces voluntary movements such as reflexes.
>
> **Efferent nerves:** Nerves that carry information from the CNS to the body.
>
> **Afferent nerves:** Nerves that carry information from the body into the CNS.
>
> **Cranial nerves:** Nerves that are connected directly to the brain.
>
> **Spinal nerves:** Nerves connected directly to the spinal cord.
>
> **Autonomic nervous system:** Regulates the body's internal environment, such as heart rate and breathing. It has three major divisions: the sympathetic nervous system, the parasympathetic nervous system, and the enteric nervous system.

The **autonomic nervous system** is predominantly controlled automatically by the brain and regulates the body's internal environment, such as your heart rate and breathing. It has three major divisions: the sympathetic nervous system, the parasympathetic nervous system, and the enteric nervous system. The enteric nervous system regulates many vital aspects of gut function. The sympathetic nervous system is often called the brain's "fight or flight" system as it prepares the body for action by increasing heart rate and blood flow to the brain and muscles, while reducing blood flow to the digestive system to save energy for other systems. It is most commonly activated by stress or danger. The parasympathetic nervous system is sometimes called the "rest and digest" system and has effects opposite to those of the sympathetic nervous system: it lowers heart rate and blood flow and supports digestion. In essence, it promotes relaxation.

Navigating the central nervous system

Scientists use specific terminology to describe locations in the brain and nervous system. Learning these will make it easier to imagine where in the brain a specific function or area is located. Medial means towards the middle, while lateral means towards the side. Anterior refers to the front, and posterior to the back. Superior means above, and inferior means below. Additionally, we use the terms rostral (towards the nose) and caudal (towards the tail). In the brain, dorsal refers to the top, while ventral refers to the bottom. However, in the spinal cord, dorsal means towards the back, and ventral means towards the front. That is because these terms are relative, meaning their location depends on the orientation of the structure that is being described. For example, the temporal lobes lie ventral to the frontal lobes, but anterior (or rostral) to the occipital lobes.

Scientists also have specific terminology when viewing brain images or cross-sections. Because the brain is a three-dimensional structure, it can be compared to a layered cake. To see its internal layers, you need to cut a slice, which reveals all the layers and fillings. Scientists perform this process in three different directions, called planes, to examine different brain areas. This process is used in neuroimaging (see Chapter 8) and anatomy studies. Imagine cutting the cake down the middle to create left and right halves; this is called the sagittal plane. The mid-sagittal plane splits the brain into two cerebral hemispheres, as shown in Figure 2.2. Cutting the cake horizontally to make a top and bottom half is known as the horizontal, or axial, plane. The third plane, called the coronal plane (from the Latin corona, meaning "crown"), divides the brain into a front (anterior) and back (posterior) section. Imagine cutting a section of the brain from ear to ear: this is the coronal plane.

Major divisions of the brain

The brain can be divided into three main parts: the cerebrum, brainstem, and cerebellum. The brainstem connects to the anterior part of the spinal cord and forms the base of the brain. It controls vital functions such as breathing, swallowing, heart rate, and sleep. The cerebellum, often called the "little brain", is located beneath the cerebrum. The cerebrum is the largest and uppermost part of the brain, and it is the visible part that we typically think of when we hear the word brain.

Cerebrum

The cerebrum consists of two halves, known as the left and right cerebral hemispheres. These two hemispheres are connected via the **corpus callosum**, a large white matter tract (see section on white matter tracts

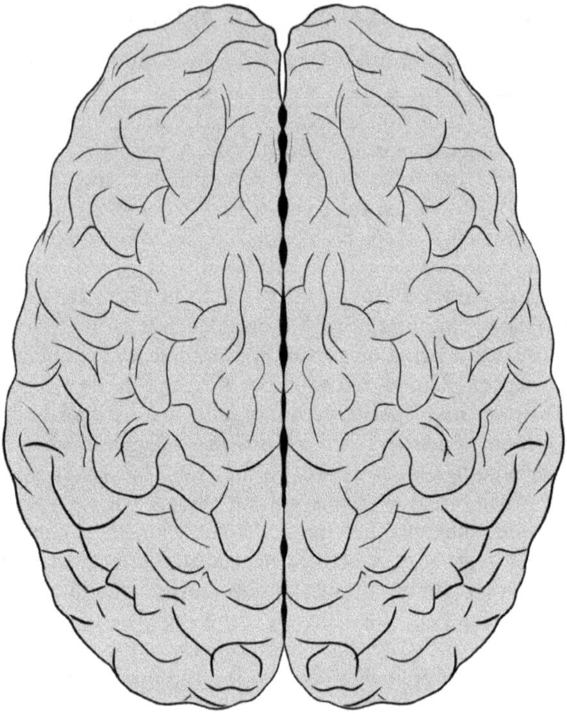

Figure 2.2 The brain viewed from a superior position (from above). The two cerebral hemispheres are clearly recognisable as they are divided by the longitudinal fissure.

below). The outermost layer of the cerebral hemispheres is the cerebral cortex, and it has a wrinkled, walnut-like, folded appearance. These folds are the result of the brain adapting to fit more surface area into a smaller space (in this case, the skull) to increase processing power. The resulting "hills" are known as **gyri** (singular: **gyrus**) and are separated by "valleys", which are called **sulci** (singular: **sulcus**), or **fissures** if they are especially deep. What is most remarkable about these folds is that they are not completely random, but so consistently similar across individual brains

> **Corpus callosum**: A large white matter tract that connects the two cerebral hemispheres.
>
> **Gyri** (singular: **gyrus**): The hills, or bumps, in the folding of the cerebral cortex.

Sulci (singular: **sulcus**)**:** The valleys, or grooves, in the folding of the cerebral cortex.

Fissure: A very deep sulcus.

Frontal lobes: Involved in executive functions, decision-making, and problem-solving.

Temporal lobes: Involved in auditory processing, visual recognition, emotion, and memory.

that they can be used as landmarks for navigation. The deepest valley, or fissure, in the brain is called the longitudinal fissure (also known as the interhemispheric fissure) and separates the brain into two halves, or cerebral hemispheres, as shown in Figure 2.2.

Using gyri and sulci as landmarks, each cerebral hemisphere can be further divided into four primary regions, or lobes, as shown in Figure 2.3. These lobes are similar in appearance on both sides of the brain, and since we have two hemispheres, we have two of each lobe. **The frontal lobe** is the largest of the brain's lobes and is situated at the front of the brain. It is separated from the rest of the brain by two distinct landmarks: the central sulcus, which marks the boundary between the frontal and parietal lobes, and the lateral fissure (also called the Sylvian fissure), which separates the frontal lobe from the temporal lobes. The frontal lobes contain three important regions: the primary motor cortex (the final exit point for neurons responsible for the body's muscles and fine motor control), the premotor cortex, and the prefrontal cortex. The frontal lobe is responsible for executive functions such as decision-making and problem-solving. The left frontal lobe (although in some individuals it is located on the right) also houses Broca's area, a region that plays a key role in language production. You can read more about this in Chapter 6.

The **temporal lobes** are separated from the frontal and parietal lobes by the lateral fissure. The primary auditory cortex is situated within the temporal lobes, and this is where sound is projected to and initially processed from the ears. The temporal lobes are also important for visual item recognition, emotional processing, and memory. **The parietal lobe** lies posterior to the frontal lobe, after the central sulcus. It is important for processing sensory information, such as touch and pain. It is also important for orienting in space and navigation (Vandenberghe et al., 2012). **The occipital lobe lies** in the back of the brain and is primarily involved in processing visual information.

The cerebral cortex is only about 3 mm thick and is organised into different layers, which represent groupings of various cell types. The much

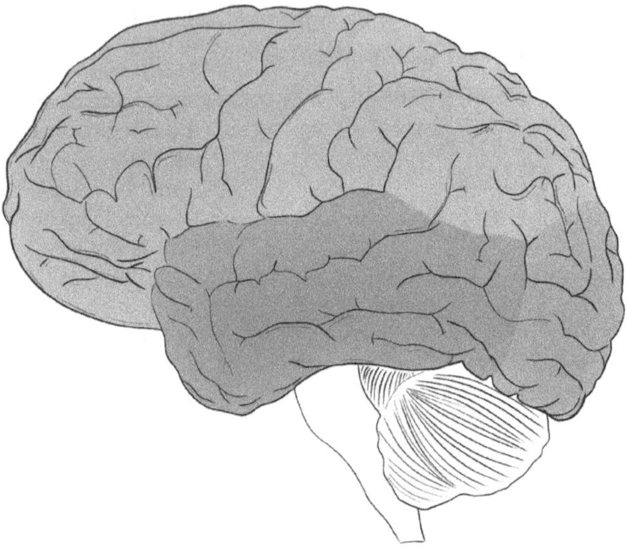

Figure 2.3 The four major lobes of the cerebral cortex: the frontal lobe in blue, the temporal lobe in purple, the parietal lobe in ochre, and the occipital lobe in pink.

> **Parietal lobes**: Involved in sensory processing (touch, pain), spatial orientation, and navigation.
>
> **Occipital lobes**: Involved in visual processing.
>
> **Cytoarchitecture**: The structural organisation of the tissue across the cortex.

larger volume beneath it consists of subcortical structures and white matter. The cerebral cortex contains six main stacked layers, and each of these layers looks slightly different as it has its own unique combination of cell types. Although most areas of the cortex contain five or six layers, the relative distribution (thickness) of these layers, as well as the size and shape within the layers, varies between brain regions. This is also referred to as **cytoarchitecture**, or the pattern of cell organisation across the cortex. German anatomist and neuropsychiatrist Korbinian Brodmann (1868–1918) studied the cytoarchitecture of the brain and used this information to divide the cerebral cortex into 52 different areas (Zilles, 2018). These areas are called Brodmann areas and are

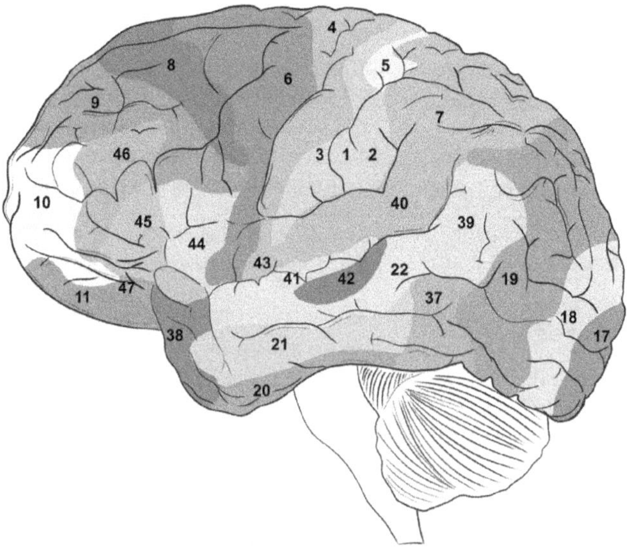

Figure 2.4 Brodmann areas visualised on the lateral surface of the left cerebral hemisphere. Not all 52 areas are shown because some are located more medially and are therefore not visible from this view.

visualised in Figure 2.4 and are one of the most influential ways of dividing the cerebral cortex. Although Brodmann's organisation was based solely on anatomy, many of these areas have also been shown to have different functional specialisations. For example, Brodmann area 17 in the occipital lobe is also known as the primary visual cortex, as this is where visual information is first processed in the brain.

Cerebellum

The cerebellum is sometimes called the "little brain" and is located inferior to the cerebrum, at the back of the brain. Although it is considerably smaller than the cerebrum, it contains more than half of the neurons of the entire nervous system. It has a folded structure, similar to the cerebral cortex, and consists of three different layers. The cerebellum is essential for movement coordination, balance, and motor control. Imagine that you want to start playing a new sport, like rugby. The cerebellum plays a crucial role in sequencing the movements you will need to be able to catch and then pass the rugby ball fluently. Damage to the cerebellum can cause cerebellar **ataxia**, which is a group of disorders that lead to problems with movement coordination, balance, and slurred speech, because of difficulties controlling the muscles involved in creating sound (Schmahmann, 2004). The cerebellum is also involved in various non-motor functions, including language processing, memory, and emotional processing.

Ataxia: A group of disorders that lead to problems with movement coordination, balance, and slurred speech because of difficulties controlling the muscles involved in creating sound.

Basal ganglia: Subcortical system important for motor control.

Nuclei: Compact clusters of grey matter that typically have similar connections and functions.

Thalamus: A subcortical structure that consists of complex clusters of nuclei that act as a routing hub.

Hypothalamus: Subcortical structure involved in a wide array of bodily functions, such as hunger, thirst, body temperature, and sexual behaviour.

Subcortical structures

Deep within the two cerebral hemispheres lie several grey matter structures that are strongly connected with each other, but also to other regions of the brain. These structures are normally grouped into systems and contribute to a wide array of behaviours. One system is the **basal ganglia**, which consists of several different **nuclei** (compact clusters of grey matter), including the caudate nucleus, the globus pallidus, and the putamen. The basal ganglia are crucial for motor control, and you will read more about this in Chapter 11.

The basal ganglia surround the **thalamus**, a pair of interconnected central structures that act as a routing hub. All sensory signals from the body (except smell) arrive in the thalamus, which then routes them to the appropriate brain regions. It has connections to almost all parts of the cortex which it sends and receives information from. These connections result in circuits called thalamocortical loops, which mainly support memory and motor functions.

The **hypothalamus** lies beneath the thalamus and has a very different role: it contains nuclei that are involved in many bodily functions, such as hunger, thirst, body temperature, and sexual behaviour. It is also the brain's main connection with the hormonal systems of the body (see Chapter 3). The hypothalamus is strongly connected to the brainstem and to the amygdala and hippocampus in the limbic system.

Another set of important subcortical structures forms the **limbic system.** The limbic system is important for processing emotional information,

Limbic system: Subcortical system that is important for processing emotional information, learning, and motivation.

Amygdala: An almond-shaped subcortical structure that plays an important role in emotional regulation.

White matter tracts: Bundles of myelinated axons in the brain that connect different areas.

learning, and motivation. Components of the system include the **amygdala,** an almond-shaped structure which plays an important role in emotional regulation, the mammillary bodies, the fornix, and the hippocampus, which all play an important role in learning and memory (Chapter 12). The thalamus and hypothalamus are also part of the limbic system. A cortical region called the cingulate gyrus, located just above the corpus callosum in each hemisphere, is usually also considered part of the limbic system and is involved in several cognitive functions, including conflict monitoring and emotional evaluation.

White matter pathways

It is also important to consider not just different brain areas, but how different areas are connected. **White matter tracts** are bundles of myelinated axons in the brain that connect different areas. There are several types of connections: projection tracts connect the cerebral cortex with other structures in the CNS, including the spinal cord. For example, the corticospinal tract connects the motor cortex with the spinal cord. This pathway is often damaged in spinal cord injuries and can lead to paralysis of different parts of the body. Association fibres (or sometimes called intrahemispheric tracts) are tracts that connect areas in the same cerebral hemisphere. One example is the arcuate fasciculus, which connects two important language areas in the brain (read more about this in Chapter 6). Lastly, commissural tracts connect areas in the two different hemispheres. The corpus callosum is both the largest commissural and the largest white matter tract in the brain, which emphasises the crucial role of information transfer across the hemispheres.

Conclusion

This chapter has given an overview of neuroanatomical vocabulary, the main structures of the human brain and their associative functions. It is hard to cover the complexity and intricacies of the brain in such a short overview, but we hope that this chapter has provided some foundational reference points when you engage with psychobiological literature.

Further reading

Additional academic source: Banich, M. T., & Compton, R. J. (2018). *Cognitive Neuroscience* (4th ed.). Cambridge University Press.

Additional academic source: Vanderah, T. W., & Gould, D. J. (2025). *Nolte's The Human Brain: An Introduction to its Functional Anatomy* (9th ed.). Elsevier.

References

Pakkenberg, B., Pelvig, D., Marner, L., Bundgaard, M. J., Gundersen, H. J. G., Nyengaard, J. R., & Regeur, L. (2003). Aging and the human neocortex. *Experimental Gerontology, 38*(1–2), 95–99. https://doi.org/10.1016/S0531-5565(02)00151-1

Schmahmann, J. D. (2004). Disorders of the cerebellum: ataxia, dysmetria of thought, and the cerebellar cognitive affective syndrome. *The Journal of Neuropsychiatry and Clinical Neurosciences, 16*(3), 367–378. https://doi.org/10.1176/jnp.16.3.367

Vandenberghe, R., Molenberghs, P., & Gillebert, C. R. (2012). Spatial attention deficits in humans: the critical role of superior compared to inferior parietal lesions. *Neuropsychologia, 50*(6), 1092–1103. https://doi.org/10.1016/j.neuropsychologia.2011.12.016

Zilles, K. (2018). Brodmann: a pioneer of human brain mapping—his impact on concepts of cortical organization. *Brain, 141*(11), 3262–3278. https://doi.org/10.1093/brain/awy273

Chapter 3

How the nervous system works

Signal generation and information transfer

Introduction

"Dopamine fasting" and other dopamine trends spread across social media platforms like they are gospel in psychobiology. Influencers and "experts" claim that dopamine is the reason you can't stop scrolling, promising increased focus, improved relationship satisfaction, and even the "rewiring of our minds" by avoiding various pleasures such as screens or different types of food and drinks. These ideas often rely on overly simplified and sometimes incorrect explanations of dopamine's role in the brain and its part in the reward system. Ironically, these ideas reveal more about social signals than about psychobiological ones.

In the brain, signals are tiny electrical-chemical messages transmitted rapidly between neurons. Neurons are designed to carry information throughout the central nervous system (CNS). This section will explore the basics of neural signalling and examine the neural subsystems that enable this communication.

Cells in the CNS

There are two main classes of cells in the nervous system: neurons and glia. Neurons carry information from one location to another and are involved in information processing. Glial cells serve supportive functions and are thought to make up about 90% of the cells in the human brain.

All neurons have, more or less, the same structure. They are made up of three parts: a cell body, dendrites, and an axon. The cell body contains the nucleus and other cell subunits that are responsible for producing proteins and enzymes that maintain cell functioning. The dendrites are the part of the neuron that receives information from neighbouring neurons. The dendrites spread out like the branches of a tree, and the shape and number of branches can vary significantly depending on neuron type. The axon is the part that sends information to other neurons.

DOI: 10.4324/9781003571537-4

The axon can vary significantly in length: some are very short and do not reach much further than the length of the cell body and dendrites. But they can also be very long and span considerable distances to reach other brain regions. The neuron can have many dendrites but only one axon. However, the single axon can extend into different branches to communicate with multiple other cells, and these branches are called **collaterals**.

> **Collaterals**: The branches that can extend from the axon to enable communication with multiple other neurons.
>
> **Sensory neurons:** Neurons that carry sensory information to the central nervous system.
>
> **Motor neurons:** Neurons that send information from the brain and spinal cord to the muscles.
>
> **Interneurons:** Neurons that connect with other neurons within the CNS.
>
> **Blood-brain barrier**: A semipermeable membrane that prevents harmful substances from entering the brain.

There are about 61–99 billion neurons in the adult human brain (Goriely, 2024) in various sizes and shapes. They can, amongst other ways, be classified according to their functions. Using this function classification system, **sensory neurons** are those that carry sensory information to the CNS. **Motor neurons** send information from the brain and spinal cord to the muscles and are responsible for movement and motor control. **Interneurons** connect neurons within the CNS and make up the majority of the neurons in the brain.

Glia cells are considered support cells, secondary to the important information-carrying system of neurons. However, glia are critical to the functioning of the nervous system (Zuchero & Barres, 2015). There are different types of glial cells, including astrocytes, oligodendrocytes, Schwann cells, and microglia. These cells have a range of functions, including providing structural support, guiding neurons during development, producing myelin, delivering nutrients to neurons, and cleaning up the CNS by removing debris and dead neurons. In addition, glia are critical for maintaining the **blood–brain barrier**, which is a semipermeable membrane that prevents harmful substances from entering the brain. The glial cells are tightly packed between the blood vessels and neurons, creating a physical barrier akin to a castle wall, keeping many drugs, toxins, immune system cells, and nutrients out of the CNS.

Electrical and chemical signalling in the CNS

Neuronal communication relies on a combination of electrical and chemical processes. This electrochemical signalling can be divided into two broad components: the electrical information transfer *within* the neuron and the chemical information transfer *between* neurons.

Information transfer within neurons

Each neuron is enclosed by a cell membrane that acts as a barrier for ions, which are electrically charged particles. When at rest, there is an electrical charge difference between the inside and outside of this membrane. This is known as the neuron's resting potential, typically around –70 mV across the membrane (with the inside being negative relative to the outside). Ions such as sodium (Na+) and potassium (K+) can pass through the cell membrane via specific channels called ion channels. Input from other neurons can cause these channels to open or close. For example, if a passive current of sufficient strength flows across the axon membrane, it can trigger the opening of voltage-gated sodium channels. This change in ion concentration reduces the negative charge inside the neuron, moving it away from its resting potential. If the cell receives enough stimulation to reach about –50 mV, a threshold is achieved, and the cell membrane becomes fully permeable, leading to firing. When the cell fires, the electrical charge inside the membrane temporarily reverses to approximately +40 mV. This process, called depolarisation, followed by repolarisation, is known as the action potential (see Figure 3.1). Repolarisation is achieved through an outward flow of potassium as the sodium channels close. During repolarisation, there is a brief hyperpolarisation period, where the inside becomes even more negative than at rest. This makes it more difficult for the axon to depolarise again immediately and also prevents the action potential from travelling backwards. Afterwards, the neuron returns to its resting potential.

Information transfer between neurons

The axon ends in a bulb-like structure called the terminal bouton, packed with tiny synaptic vesicles, small balloon-like packages filled with neurotransmitters that are ready to relay messages to the next neuron. This location is where the electrical signal transforms into a chemical message. Between each neuron is a small gap, called a **synaptic cleft**. When the

Synaptic cleft: The gap between two neurons, where they communicate.

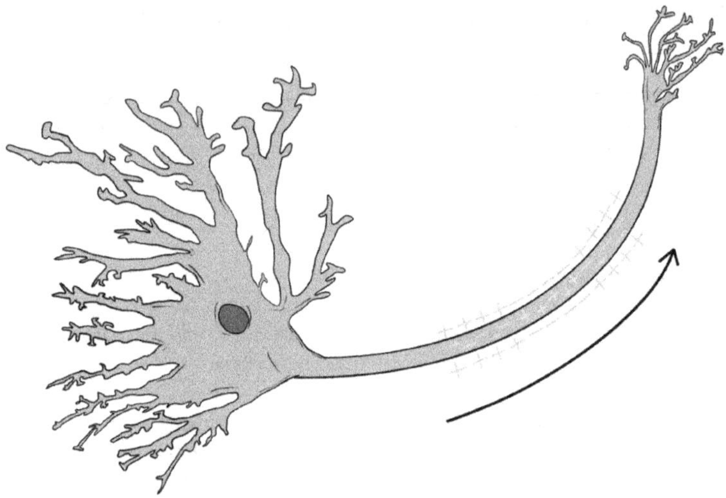

Figure 3.1 The conduction of the action potential. The figure shows how an action potential travels down the axon as a wave of depolarisation, while the area behind repolarises.

> **Synapse:** The structure that includes the presynaptic terminal (terminal boutons), the synaptic cleft, and the postsynaptic membrane.

action potential reaches the end of the axon terminal, it triggers a sequence of events that releases neurotransmitters into the synaptic cleft. The process is like dropping a spoonful of powdered cocoa into a cup of hot milk: the molecules spread across the synapse, carrying the message towards the next neuron. The neuron that releases the neurotransmitter is called the presynaptic neuron, and the connected neuron is called the postsynaptic neuron. The **synapse** is made up of three components: the presynaptic terminal (terminal boutons), the synaptic cleft, and the postsynaptic membrane.

The neurotransmitters will bind with receptors in the postsynaptic membrane of the dendrite in the postsynaptic neuron (this is also called the binding site). This will consequently change the electrical charge of the postsynaptic neuron in the small area of the receptor site and lead to an alteration in the flow of ions across the cell membrane. This is when the chemical signal is transformed back into an electrical signal. Some neurotransmitters, such as gamma-aminobutyric acid (GABA), will have an **inhibitory effect**: meaning that they make the inside more negative, decreasing

> **Inhibitory effect**: Making the neuron less likely to fire.
>
> **Excitatory effect**: Making the neuron more likely to fire.
>
> **Postsynaptic potential**: The local change in electrical potential.

the chance for an action potential to occur. Other neurotransmitters, such as acetylcholine, have an **excitatory effect**, making the neuron more likely to fire. However, the effect is not only determined by the neurotransmitter type but also by the kind of receptor it binds to in the postsynaptic membrane. The local change in electrical potential is called a **postsynaptic potential**. These are normally small in magnitude and weaken with the distance they have to travel to the start of the axon (an area called the axon hillock). Therefore, a single synapse rarely sparks an action potential on its own. Instead, action potentials usually arise from the combined activity of multiple inputs. Imagine that the axon hillock is like a reservoir at the bottom of a mountain: small streams (signals) flow down from nearby hills with full force, while streams from distant hills slow down, contributing only a small trickle to the reservoir. The reservoir overflows (action potential fires) only when the combined water from all streams is sufficient to reach the tipping point.

Neurotransmitters

Neurotransmitters are the chemicals that neurons release to communicate with one another. There are many different types of neurotransmitters, and they influence neural transmission in different ways. There are both inhibitory and excitatory neurotransmitters, and you may wonder why both types are needed? Think of it as riding a bike: we could rely only on the pedals, first to increase our speed and then stop pedalling to slow down. But sometimes, we may have to make a very sudden stop (if a cat jumps out in front of the bike) or in a precise place (next to a cute dog you want to pet). The CNS needs to be able to quickly ramp up or ramp down activity in a similar fashion.

One class of neurotransmitter is amino acids, the smallest building blocks of proteins. The two main ones in the CNS are glutamate (which has an excitatory effect) and GABA, which is the main inhibitory neurotransmitter. Glutamate is used at approximately 20% of synapses in the CNS. It is involved in learning and memory, amongst other things. Too much glutamate can cause excitotoxicity, in which excessive activity at the receptor can lead to cell death because of too much stimulation. In

Indirect agonist: A substance that enhances the effect of a neurotransmitter without directly binding to its receptor.

contrast, GABA is the main inhibitory neurotransmitter in the CNS. There are different GABA receptors in the brain, and although they work in slightly different ways, they all make neurons less likely to fire. Alcohol is one example of a substance that interacts with GABA: it acts as an **indirect agonist**. Rather than binding at GABA's usual site, it attaches elsewhere on the receptor and increases GABA's effect, making the receptor more responsive. This produces the relaxation and reduced stress or anxiety often associated with drinking. With repeated or heavy drinking, the brain builds tolerance: it downregulates GABA receptors and increases excitatory signalling to compensate. This imbalance can be noticed once the effects of the alcohol wear off: the hangover. Ever noticed that hangovers most often mean increased stress, anxiety, shakiness, or racing thoughts? Hangovers are essentially a mini-withdrawal caused by an imbalance of neurotransmitters in the brain, among other things (Ngui et al., 2022).

Neurotransmitter systems

The other main neurotransmitters in the CNS are organised into networks of neurons that produce, release, and respond to specific neurotransmitters. These are mainly produced by neurons with cell bodies subcortically or in the brainstem and project all over the brain. The extensive reach of these networks means that they influence many different behaviours.

Acetylcholine (Ach) is the neurotransmitter used in the cholinergic system. This system is involved in several vital functions, including attention, memory, and regulating sleep–wake cycles. Serotonin is the neurotransmitter released by the serotonergic system. It can lead to either an excitatory or inhibitory response, depending on the receptor subtype. The system influences many things, including mood regulation. Some of the most popular drugs to combat depression are known as selective serotonin reuptake inhibitors (SSRIs), which increase serotonin levels in the synaptic cleft. But because serotonin affects so many systems, taking SSRIs can come with unwanted side effects, such as sleep disruptions, killing your appetite, or dampening sexual motivation (e.g. libido) and performance.

Dopamine is the main neurotransmitter in the dopaminergic system, which is important for attention, learning, reward processing, planning, and working memory. This system is organised into pathways based on the origin and target of dopamine projections, including the mesolimbic, mesocortical, nigrostriatal, and tuberoinfundibular pathways. There are different types of dopamine receptors in the brain: some enhance neuronal signalling, while others reduce it. Noradrenaline, also known as norepinephrine, is the main neurotransmitter in the noradrenergic system. The noradrenergic system affects attention and arousal, including sleep. The noradrenergic system and cholinergic system have a large functional overlap. This is because many neurotransmitter systems are highly interrelated. For example, both noradrenaline and dopamine systems are thought to be disrupted in attention deficit hyperactivity disorder (ADHD). Individuals with ADHD can have difficulty sustaining attention, following instructions, organising tasks, controlling impulses, and more. A common ADHD medication is methylphenidate, and it is thought to block reuptake of both noradrenaline and dopamine in the synaptic cleft, meaning that it increases the levels of these neurotransmitters in the brain.

Hormones

Hormones are chemical messengers secreted by cells that travel through the bloodstream to act on specific target tissues, including the brain. Many hormones are produced by endocrine glands, which come in many shapes and sizes throughout the body. They can be broadly classified into three types: peptide hormones, amine hormones, or steroid hormones. Amine and peptide hormones bind to receptors on the cell membrane, while steroid hormones can pass through the cell membrane and bind to receptors located inside the cell. Hormones generally act much more slowly than action potentials. Some hormones can act almost immediately, while others take minutes, hours, or even days.

Hormones influence neuronal activity in several ways: they can alter neural excitability, making action potentials more or less likely to occur. They can also influence synaptic transmission by, amongst other things, modulating release, uptake, or even synthesis of neurotransmitters. At the same time, neuronal signalling regulates hormone release through brain circuits such as the hypothalamic–pituitary axis. This creates a continuous feedback loop, allowing the brain and body to communicate and adjust to changing conditions. These interactions affect several physiological processes. For example, oxytocin is often called the "bonding hormone" as it has been linked to social bonding and trust and plays a large role in how we interact with other people. Hormones can also modify physical characteristics and brain function. For example, taking hormones to induce physical changes that align with a person's gender identity is a key part of gender-affirming hormone therapy. Beyond the physical effects and improvements in quality of life, researchers are also investigating how altering hormone levels can influence brain structure and function.

Conclusion

The nervous system communicates using a combination of electrical signals and chemical messengers. These signals, together with hormones that influence both brain and body, form the foundation of how we think, feel, and respond to our environment. Understanding these mechanisms is essential for advancing our knowledge of brain function and its influence on behaviours.

Further reading

Additional academic source: Nelson, R. J., & Kriegsfeld, L. J. (2022). *An Introduction to Behavioral Endocrinology* (6th ed.). Oxford University Press/Sinauer Associates.

Related podcast: https://www.brainsciencepodcast.com/, the podcast Brain Science explores different topics about how the brain works and how it relates to behaviour. Episode eight is specifically about how neurons communicate.

Related film: *Lucy* (2014). Follows a woman who, after accidentally absorbing a powerful synthetic drug, begins unlocking increasingly vast portions of her brain, gaining extraordinary abilities that transform her into a superhuman force.

References

Goriely, A. (2024). Eighty-six billion and counting: do we know the number of neurons in the human brain? *Brain,* awae390. https://doi.org/10.1093/brain/awae390

Ngui, H. H. L., Kow, A. S. F., Lai, S., Tham, C. L., Ho, Y. C., & Lee, M. T. (2022). Alcohol withdrawal and the associated mood disorders—a review. *International Journal of Molecular Sciences, 23*(23), 14912. https://doi.org/10.3390/ijms232314912

Zuchero, J. B., & Barres, B. A. (2015). Glia in mammalian development and disease. *Development, 142*(22), 3805. https://doi.org/10.1242/dev.129304

Section 2

Key theories

This section aims to provide an overview of key theoretical principles that informed psychobiological research. It will discuss neural plasticity as a core principle across many areas of psychobiology, as well as network neuroscience.

At the end of section two, you will:

- Know why understanding neural plasticity is critical for understanding learning and the impact of environmental factors on the nervous system
- Have learned about Hebbian learning theory and other processes relevant for neural plasticity
- Have gained knowledge of how the representation of psychological functions in the brain can be understood from a network perspective

DOI: 10.4324/9781003571537-5

Chapter 4

How the brain changes itself

Neural plasticity as a core principle in psychobiology

Introduction

The human brain is one of the most complex things in the known universe. It is estimated to consist of about 61 to 99 billion neurons (Goriely, 2024) and billions of other cells, such as glial cells. In contrast, the number of protein-coding genes in the human genome is much smaller: about 20,000. These numbers make it clear that the structure and function of the brain are not solely determined by genetic factors. In addition, the so-called **exposome** (Ibanez et al., 2024), the sum of all external exposures to environmental factors a person encounters in their lifetime, also plays a crucial role in how our brains function. The exposome encompasses not only to the physical environment but also includes a wide variety of societal, economic, lifestyle, pollution, and other factors.

The environment shapes our brain's structure and function from the very beginning of our lives. Imagine two babies: one born in Gothenburg, Sweden, the other one born in Edinburgh, Scotland. Because the Swedish child grows up in a Swedish-speaking family, the brain's language networks will be assembled differently from those of the English-speaking Scottish child. As adults, the Swedish child will speak fluent Swedish, while the Scottish child will not. While the genome provides a blueprint for the relevant brain structures necessary for being able to learn a language (as learning Swedish or English requires the same language network in the brain), the specific language is not encoded in the genes but is fully determined by the environment. In addition to spoken language, the brains of the two people will show myriads of other tiny differences based on what they learned from their parents and in school, which hobbies they choose to pursue, which friends they spend time with, and so on.

Exposome: The sum of external exposures to environmental factors a person encounters in their lifetime.

DOI: 10.4324/9781003571537-6

Learning something new: the role of neural plasticity in learning and memory

When was the last time you learned something new and exciting? The human brain has an extraordinary capability to learn new things. There are more than 7000 different languages we can learn, over 8000 types of sports to take up in our free time, and tens of thousands of different jobs we can pursue. Any of these can be mastered from the ground up by someone with no prior experience. With enough time and motivation, it is possible for most people to learn how to surf, how to speak Swedish, or become a professional woodcrafter. The reason why the human brain can learn such a staggering variety of skills is that fact that they are not genetically hardwired at birth, but that learning skills elicits a phenomenon called **neural plasticity**. Neural plasticity refers to the fact that the brain can reorganise itself on the synaptic, structural, and connectional levels through various processes in response to learning something new or adapting to new circumstances. For a long time, scientists believed that the brain only learned new skills easily during early childhood "sensitive periods". Today, we know that the brain can adapt and rewire itself throughout life, even if learning or recovery may become slower with age. The idea of neural plasticity is one of the key theories in psychobiology and is of crucial importance for understanding the psychology of adaptation, experience, learning, and memory. Brain plasticity has been shown in response to learning to play a new musical instrument (Münte et al., 2002), exercise, language learning, training new skills, and many other things. A topic that has recently been in the focus of neural plasticity research is pregnancy. For example, a neuroimaging study examining changes in brain structure during pregnancy reported a large amount of adaptive, hormone-driven neuroanatomical changes in the brain (Pritschet et al., 2024). Primarily, pregnancy was associated with enhanced white matter microstructure, accompanied by reductions in grey matter, which were associated with steroid hormone changes. The scientists suggested that these changes fine-tune the brain for motherhood, for example, by optimising reactions to visual or auditory cues from the infant and promoting maternal behaviour. In the following sections, we highlight the most important forms of neural plasticity in the human brain, starting with synaptic plasticity.

> **Neural plasticity**: The ability of the brain to reorganise itself on the synaptic and other levels in response to learning a new skill or adapting to new circumstances.

One of the most important forms of neural plasticity is **synaptic plasticity**, which refers to the fact that the synapses that connect neurons strengthen when the neurons are active together and weaken when they do not share activity. The theoretical basis for synaptic plasticity is called **Hebbian learning** after Donald Olding Hebb (1904–1985), a Canadian scientist who introduced the idea that neurons that fire together (are active together), wire together (form a stronger synaptic connection) (Hebb, 1949). There are two main processes underlying synaptic plasticity: one called **long-term potentiation (LTP)** and the other **long-term depression (LTD)** (Malenka & Bear, 2004). LTP is a persistent, activity-dependent increase in synaptic strength following synchronous activity of two connected neurons. LTD has nothing to do with the mental health disorder depression and represents the opposite of LTP. Specifically, LTD is a persistent decrease in synaptic strength following inactivity of two connected neurons. Together, LTP and LTD are crucial processes for learning and memory in the brain as they allow for an efficient use of brain tissue to learn new skills throughout life.

Synaptic plasticity: The synapses that connect different neurons which each other are modulated in an activity-dependent way. If the neurons are active together, the synapses get strengthened, if they are not active together, they get weakened.

Hebbian learning: The idea that the neural basis of learning is that neurons that fire together (are active together), wire together (form a stronger synaptic connection).

Long-term potentiation (LTP): A persistent, activity-dependent increase in synaptic strength following synchronous activity of two connected neurons.

Long-term depression (LTD): A persistent decrease in synaptic strength following inactivity of two connected neurons.

Learning a new skill can reshape the brain not only at the level of the synapse but also in size and shape of entire brain structures. This type of **structural plasticity** has famously been documented in the grey matter density of the hippocampus of licensed London taxi drivers (Griesbauer et al., 2022). The hippocampus is a core structure in memory (see Chapter 12). The taxi drivers must memorise about 26,000 street names and thousands of points of interest in London, a demanding spatial memory task. This training leads to substantial structural changes in the hippocampus, increasing grey matter density in the posterior part while decreasing it in the anterior part. Beyond structural plasticity in

Structural plasticity: Neural plasticity can lead to structural changes in the brain, such as alterations in the size or shape of grey matter areas, white matter tracts, or changes in dendritic spines.

Molecular plasticity: Neural plasticity can lead to changes in molecular processes such as gene expression and protein synthesis in the brain.

grey matter, activities such as exercise or learning a new language have also been shown to lead to neuroplastic changes in white matter, which connects different brain areas. Finally, there is also **molecular plasticity**, which can lead to changes in molecular processes such as gene expression and protein synthesis in the brain.

Compensating for what is lost: the role of neural plasticity in recovery from brain injury

Neural plasticity plays a major role not only in learning new skills but also in recovery after brain injury. Each year, more than 300,000 people in the UK are admitted to hospitals with brain injuries caused by car accidents, strokes, cancer, brain inflammation, and other reasons. While some people make a full recovery, many are left with permanent damage. Despite initial impairments, many still improve in cognitive and motor functions over time. While part of this recovery may stem from the gradual reduction of bleeding or swelling in the injured brain, compensatory processes driven by neural plasticity also play a key role. For example, if someone suffers a stroke in Broca's area, the main language production region located in the left inferior frontal lobe, they often experience difficulties with speech. Over time, this impairment can sometimes improve as associated cortical areas take over parts of the damaged area's function. Neuropsychologists can try to foster these processes by specially training communication abilities that rely on other brain areas, such as sign language. However, a general principle is that compensatory mechanisms get less efficient with age. A young child who suffers brain damage often regains more function than an adult with a similar injury. There are even case reports of young children who underwent hemispherectomy (the surgical removal of a whole brain hemisphere, a rare surgery performed to treat severe epilepsy that cannot be controlled for by medication) and years later show relatively unimpaired language and motor functions, as their remaining hemisphere rewired substantially to take over the lost functions. If an adult lost an entire hemisphere, they would most likely be unable to regain the functions of the missing half. These extreme cases of neural plasticity in young people show how truly exceptional neural plasticity can shape our brains. Another fascinating example of reorganisation due to neural plasticity occurs in the visual brain areas of blind people. Although these areas receive no neural input from the eyes, they do not remain idle. Instead, the begin processing non-visual input such as auditory information, a remarkable reorganisation that maximises the usage of the brain's functional capacity.

The dark side of neural plasticity: maladaptation

Does neural plasticity always produce a positive result, such as new skills and memories? Unfortunately, the answer is no. Neural plasticity refers simply to processes in which the brain reorganises itself in response to experiences or environmental changes. As such, neural plasticity is a process that is neutral with respect to whether its outcomes are positive or negative. Therefore, while many changes driven by neural plasticity are adaptive (helpful and positive), it can also lead to **maladaptive** (e.g., harmful and negative) outcomes.

One example of a maladaptive outcome due to neural plasticity is chronic pain. Imagine someone has a bike accident after coming home from a party and injures their knee. In the first moments, the injury causes intense pain, and the person will likely receive strong painkillers to manage it. However, if the pain is poorly managed and persists over a longer period, it may become chronic since pain receptor cells fire too much. This can lead not only to plastic reorganisation of pain networks themselves but also of pain-related perceptual and emotion networks. As a result, it often makes the person highly sensitive and aware of pain, and they may still experience it even a long time after the actual injury has healed. For some people, chronic pain can even persist after an arm or a leg has been amputated due to the reorganisation of cortical networks – a phenomenon that has been referred to as phantom pain. A further common example of a maladaptation due to neural plasticity is tinnitus (e.g., people hearing a ringing sound in the ear, even though there is no external sound source). Because the phantom noise is heard so often, connections between neurons in auditory structures in the brain are enhanced, leading to a higher probability of spontaneous firing, which increases the tinnitus problem.

Maladaptations due to brain plasticity can also play a role in hearing loss. For example, if someone experiences increasing hearing issues, they are often prescribed hearing aids to improve auditory function. However, if they do not use

> **Maladaptation**: Negative or harmful consequences of neural plasticity processes.

the hearing aids, activity in the auditory areas of the brain decreases due to the limited input. This reduction in neurons firing together can weaken synapses in the auditory cortex or trigger structural changes, potentially worsening the hearing problems. Neuropsychologists often describe these and similar processes with the phrase "use it or lose it". In other words, when a brain region is not used regularly, there may be negative functional and structural changes.

Conclusion

Without neural plasticity, we would be unable to learn a foreign language or excel in a new sport. It is a core principle underlying much psychobiological research on learning and memory and is crucial for recovery after brain damage from stroke or injuries. While neural plasticity often produces positive outcomes, it can also lead to maladaptive effects.

Further reading

Additional academic source: Denes, G. (2016). *Neural Plasticity Across the Lifespan*. How the brain can change. Routledge.

Related documentary: *The brain that changes itself* (2008). A documentary about neuroplasticity.

Related information video: *Neuroplasticity: How to rewire your brain* (BBC, 2022). https://www.bbc.com/reel/video/p098v92g/neuroplasticity-how-to-rewire-your-brain

Relevant web article: *Meet the 'glass-half-full girl' whose brain rewired after losing a hemisphere* (2023). https://www.npr.org/sections/health-shots/2023/03/22/1165131907/neuroplasticity-plasticity-glass-half-full-girl

References

Goriely, A. (2025). Eighty-six billion and counting: do we know the number of neurons in the human brain? *Brain, 148*, 689–691. https://doi.org/10.1093/brain/awae390

Griesbauer, E. M., Manley, E., Wiener, J. M., & Spiers, H. J. (2022). London taxi drivers: a review of neurocognitive studies and an exploration of how they build their cognitive map of London. *Hippocampus, 32*, 3–20. https://doi.org/10.1002/hipo.23395

Hebb, D. O. (1949). *The Organization of Behavior. A Neuropsychological Theory.* John Wiley and sons, Inc.

Ibanez, A., Melloni, L., Świeboda, P., Hynes, W., Ikiz, B., Ayadi, R., Thioye, M., Walss-Bass, C., Güntekin, B., Mishra, J., Salama, M., Dunlop, S., Duran-Aniotz, C., & Eyre, H. A. (2024). Neuroecological links of the exposome and One Health. *Neuron, 112*, 1905–1910. https://doi.org/10.1016/j.neuron.2024.04.016

Malenka, R. C., & Bear, M. F. (2004). LTP and LTD: an embarrassment of riches. *Neuron, 44*, 5–21. https://doi.org/10.1016/j.neuron.2004.09.012

Münte, T. F., Altenmüller, E., & Jäncke, L. (2002). The musician's brain as a model of neuroplasticity. *Nature Reviews. Neuroscience, 3*, 473–478. https://doi.org/10.1038/nrn843

Pritschet, L, Taylor, C. M., Cossio, D., Faskowitz, J., Santander, T., Handwerker, D. A., Grotzinger, H., Layher, E., Chrastil, E. R., & Jacobs, E. G. (2024). Neuroanatomical changes observed over the course of a human pregnancy. *Nature Neuroscience, 27*, 2253–2260. https://doi.org/10.1038/s41593-024-01741-0

Chapter 5

Connection is everything

Network theory and graph theory in psychobiology

Introduction

In the third section, you will explore how different parts of the brain can be crucial for certain functions. For example, Broca's area is essential for speaking, and damage to it can make talking difficult. While it is certainly true that specific regions are important for various tasks, it's now widely recognised that single brain areas rarely control a cognitive ability completely on their own. Instead, many different brain areas work together in complex, interconnected networks to support our thinking and actions. The exciting field of **network neuroscience** is growing quickly, aiming to understand the brain's structure and functions through a connected network perspective. This chapter explores how different brain regions collaborate to carry out specific tasks and how scientists map, record, and study the connections within the brain. In this chapter, you will learn about the basics of network theory, important terms, and about key networks in the brain.

The human connectome

The nervous system is a complex network of interconnected neurons and synapses that can be explored on many different scales. At the nanoscale, scientists zoom in on the molecular interactions that shape communication at the synapse. At the microscale, scientists examine individual neurons and the connections they form. Moving to the mesoscale, scientists study how groups of neurons work together. In most of psychobiology, the focus is on the macroscale, in which scientists investigate different brain regions and the bundle of fibres that link them.

> **Network neuroscience:** An emerging field that tries to understand brain structure and function from a network perspective.

DOI: 10.4324/9781003571537-7

Together, these various levels of organisation contribute to the **connectome**, the detailed map of all the neural connections that form the brain's complete wiring diagram. There are different types of connections, or connectivity, that scientists examine in the brain. **Structural connectivity** refers to the physical connections within the brain. These are the white matter pathways that connect different brain areas. They are relatively stable at any given time point but can change when measured over longer periods, such as during development or due to neural plasticity when learning something new (see Chapter 4). **Functional connectivity** refers to functional relationships between brain regions. In other words, it examines which regions activate together. Scientists determine functional connectivity by examining how activity in different brain regions relates over time, for example, during a task or at rest. Functional connectivity is dynamic and time-dependent. Although it describes co-activation between regions, it does not imply a causal relationship. Instead, **effective connectivity** describes the causal effects that one brain area or system has on another. There are many ways of examining connectivity in the brain. In psychobiology, the most common techniques are diffusion-weighted imaging (Chapter 8), functional magnetic resonance imaging (Chapter 8), the electroencephalogram (Chapter 7), and the magnetoencephalogram (Chapter 7).

> **Connectome:** The detailed map of all the neural connections that form the brain's complete wiring diagram.
>
> **Functional connectivity:** Refers to functional relationships between regions within the brain. In other words, it examines which regions activate together.
>
> **Structural connectivity:** Refers to the physical connections (infrastructure) within the brain.
>
> **Effective connectivity:** Describes causal effects of one system on another.

Foundations of network theory

Just like you have a social network of people you are connected to, brain areas are also part of networks. **Neural networks** are groups of connected brain areas that work together to achieve a common goal. These areas may or may not be located close to one another. In psychobiology, we use a powerful tool called **graph theory,** the mathematical study of relationships between objects. It provides tools to represent these relationships as graphs. A graph consists of two elements: **nodes** are the fundamental processing

Neural networks: Groups of connected brain areas that work together to achieve a common goal.

Graph theory: The mathematical study of networks or graphs.

Nodes: The fundamental unit of a graph, represented as circles in a diagram.

Edges: The connections between nodes in a graph, represented as lines in a diagram.

units, and **edges** are the connections between the nodes. Graph theory is not only used in psychology but also appears in countless other fields of science. In fact, you have probably already come across it today without knowing so. Perhaps you wanted to drive to the supermarket and use a navigation system to figure out the quickest way? When your GPS finds the fastest route to the supermarket, it is using graph theory to map roads and intersections into the most efficient path. Or perhaps a new friend suggestion popped up on a social media platform? Again, social media platforms use graph theory to map how people are connected and can then predict the people you may know based on your connections. A graph is therefore any network that can help us define and visualise relationships between components, and in psychobiology, these are the different brain areas and the relationships between them. A visual representation of diagrams showing different neural networks represented as brain graphs can be seen in Figure 5.1.

Edges are the representations of connectivity between the nodes. Nodes in psychobiology can be many different things. The brain differs from other natural or technological networks because it is a highly complex structure without clear boundaries between areas. For example, imagine a graph representing a music festival: the stages are the nodes, and the paths between them are the edges. In this case, the boundaries between stages and paths are clear. In contrast, brain areas and neuronal populations are harder to define. Neurons are arranged in an unknown number of anatomically distinct regions, with definitions of what constitutes a region constantly evolving. Researchers divide the brain in many ways, ranging from roughly 100 regions (50 per hemisphere) to sometimes more than 1,000! A large-scale initiative called the Human Connectome Project (HCP) was launched in 2011 and aims to map all human brain connections. The project provides free open-access datasets that scientists can use to investigate a wide array of questions about brain structure and function. Using HCP data, a group of scientists developed the HCP-MMP1 atlas, which divides the cerebral cortex into 360 distinct

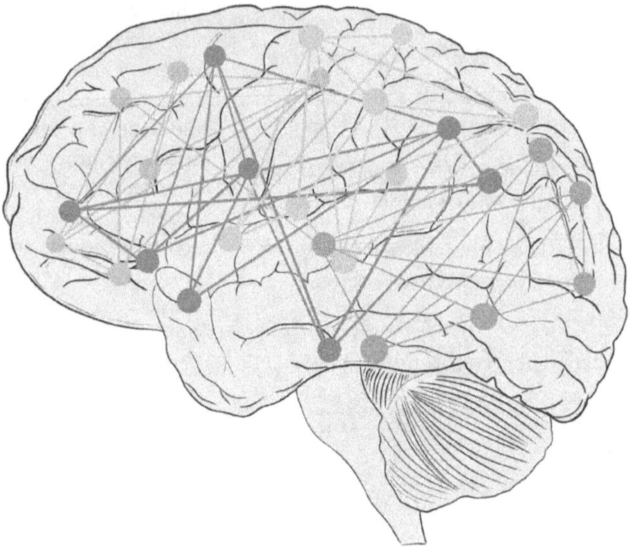

Figure 5.1 The figure shows different brain networks as graphs. Circles represent nodes, and lines represent connections between them (edges). Each network is shown in a different colour. Networks are not completely isolated and can share nodes.

regions (Glasser et al., 2016). By having access to all the data provided by the HCP, they were able to integrate structural, functional, and connectivity information to build their atlas for studying the brain.

Mapping brain networks

A major reason why network neuroscience has grown so fast is the development of different methods that can measure a wide range of elements and relationships within networks (Bassett & Sporns, 2017). Representing the brain as a graph makes it possible to study many different things. In the simplest form, we can explore where connections exist in a network. An edge is only drawn if there's a link between regions, and not all nodes will have edges connecting them. Think of it like an interconnected road system: some cities are linked via direct roads, while others are not. We can also go a step further and assign different weights to connections to show which areas are more strongly linked. This is represented by varying the thickness of the edges: thicker lines represent stronger connections, while thinner lines indicate weaker ones. Imagine how some cities have motorways connecting them, symbolising strong links, while others are connected only by smaller country roads. Additionally, scientists can examine directionality in networks, which shows the direction of connections. Some connections are bidirectional, allowing information to travel both ways, while others are one-way, like a one-way street, letting information flow in only one direction. Most studies in psychobiology focus on simple or weighted networks, since understanding the directionality remains a challenge with our current methods.

Graph analysis can also show different features of brain networks. Some studies look at how strong connections are between regions, others examine how the nodes are organised, and some explore the importance of specific nodes and what might happen if they are removed. This is especially relevant in clinical research, where scientists investigate how damage to the brain affects network structure. We are constantly learning more about brain networks, and network analysis keeps improving as technology advances. This evolving field promises many new discoveries in the future.

Networks in the brain

Have you ever heard of the urban myth that we use only 10% of our brains? This idea is wrong, as much more than 10% of the brain is active at any given time. In fact, there are even networks that are active in your brain when you do nothing in particular! The most famous one is called the default mode network (DMN) and is a set of connected regions that are active together when you, for example, daydream or when your mind wanders. It consists of many different brain regions (see Table 5.1) and even different subnetworks that perform various functions, including episodic memory (recalling past experiences), social cognition (the processing of information related to other people and social situations), and semantic (meaning) and narrative aspects of language processing. The DMN is thought to integrate different cognitive domains, creating a coherent internal narrative of our experiences, which results in internal reflection of our feelings and experiences, daydreaming, and mind wandering, amongst other things (Menon, 2023). Intriguingly, research has shown that even our friendships may be reflected in our brain networks. One study examining real-world social networks found that close friends have much more similar patterns of resting activity in the DMN (Hyon et al., 2020). This finding suggests that people who share similar values, beliefs, and ways of seeing the world may also process experiences in similar ways in their brains. Therefore, your brain might have more in common with your best friend's than you think.

Scientists have identified many networks within the brain. Since the DMN is heavily involved in rest and quiet wakefulness, activity in the DMN

Table 5.1 Some of the Major Functional Networks in the Brain and Their Associated Tasks and Regions

Network	*Primary function(s)*	*Key region(s)*
Default mode network (DMN)	Active at rest, or wakeful resting. Involved in mind wandering, self-reflection, daydreaming, reflecting over the past or the future	Posterior cingulate cortex, medial prefrontal cortex, anterior temporal cortex, angular gyrus
Dorsal attention network (DAN)	Enables you to direct and maintain attention on tasks	Intraparietal sulcus, frontal eye fields
Frontoparietal network (FPN)	Important in thinking, decision-making, and problem-solving	Dorsolateral prefrontal cortex, lateral posterior parietal cortex
Salience network (SN)	Directs attention to salient (hence the name) and important information around you. Also acts as a switch between networks at rest (DMN) and at focus (like the FPN)	Anterior insula, dorsal anterior cingulate cortex
Sensorimotor network (SN)	Integrates sensory information with motor information and controls deliberate movements	Precentral gyrus (primary motor cortex), postcentral gyrus (primary somatosensory cortex), premotor cortex
Ventral attention network (VAN)	Shift attention to unexpected, new, or important things in your environment	Temporoparietal junction, ventral frontal cortex
Visual network (VN)	Processes aspects of visual information, such as motion, shape, colour, and more	Occipital cortex

decreases during many tasks that require focused, goal-directed behaviour. The salience network (SN) is a different network that helps regulate this shift by acting as a switch between internally oriented (DMN) and externally focused executive networks, such as the dorsal attention network (DAN) or the frontoparietal network (FPN). Some networks handle specific tasks, while others help with many different tasks. For example, the visual network is highly specialised for processing visual information, while the FPN supports a wide range of cognitive tasks, such as thinking, decision-making, and problem-solving. It acts as a flexible hub, coordinating information from multiple brain regions to enable goal-directed behaviour (actions that are deliberately planned and carried out).

Consequences of network disruption

Network analyses can also help scientists understand neurological and psychiatric disorders as they can examine how different parts of the brain communicate, or fail to speak, with each other. Schizophrenia is a mental health disorder that affects how people think and experience reality, as well as behaviours such as speech and emotion. It is often associated with hallucinations (seeing or hearing things that are not there) and delusions (strong beliefs that do not match reality). There is no single cause of schizophrenia, although the condition is thought to arise from a combination of genetic and environmental factors. By studying brain networks in individuals with schizophrenia, scientists consistently find abnormal communication within and between key networks such as the DMN, SN, and FPN (Harikumar et al., 2023). When these networks cannot communicate efficiently, the brain struggles to regulate attention, switch between internal and external focus, and maintain stable representations of the world. These disruptions can help explain symptoms such as hallucinations, delusions, and disorganised thinking. It can also help us understand how different variations in network communication can give rise to variations and severity in symptoms.

Conclusion

Network neuroscience studies how the brain works as a connected system and how this shapes our thoughts, behaviours, and abilities. This method has advanced our understanding of how disruption in brain systems influences behaviour. As new methods and brain-imaging techniques continue to develop, the field is just beginning to show its full potential in advancing our understanding of the brain.

Further reading

Additional academic source: Fornito, A., Zalesky, A., & Bullmore, E. (2016). *Fundamentals of Brain Network Analysis*. Academic Press.

Additional academic source: Sporns, O. (2016). *Networks of the Brain*. MIT press.

Related podcast: Brain Inspired Podcast, episode 76 titled *Olaf Sporns: Network Neuroscience*.

Relevant web source: https://humanconnectome.org/, the website of the Human Connectome Project (HCP).

References

Bassett, D. S., & Sporns, O. (2017). Network neuroscience. *Nature Neuroscience*, *20*(3), 353–364. https://doi.org/10.1038/nn.4502

Glasser, M. F., Coalson, T. S., Robinson, E. C., Hacker, C. D., Harwell, J., Yacoub, E., Ugurbil, K., Andersson, J., Beckmann, C. F., Jenkinson, M., Smith, S. M., & Van Essen, D. C. (2016). A multi-modal parcellation of human cerebral cortex. *Nature, 536*(7615), 171–178. https://doi.org/10.1038/nature18933

Harikumar, A., Solovyeva, K. P., Misiura, M., Iraji, A., Plis, S. M., Pearlson, G. D., Turner, J. A., & Calhoun, V. D. (2023). Revisiting functional dysconnectivity: a review of three model frameworks in schizophrenia. *Current Neurology and Neuroscience Reports, 23*(12), 937–946. https://doi.org/10.1007/s11910-023-01325-8

Hyon, R., Youm, Y., Kim, J., Chey, J., Kwak, S., & Parkinson, C. (2020). Similarity in functional brain connectivity at rest predicts interpersonal closeness in the social network of an entire village. *Proceedings of the National Academy of Sciences, 117*(52), 33149–33160. https://doi.org/10.1073/pnas.2013606117

Menon, V. (2023). 20 years of the default mode network: a review and synthesis. *Neuron, 111*(16), 2469–2487. https://doi.org/10.1016/j.neuron.2023.04.023

Section 3

Key methodologies

This section aims to highlight the remarkable variety of methodologies used in psychobiological research. These include studies on brain lesions, measures of electrical and magnetic activity in the brain, neuroimaging techniques, genetic approaches, psychophysiological measurements in the peripheral nervous system, and neurostimulation methods.
At the end of section three, you will:

- Know about the important historical role of lesion studies in psychobiology
- Have learned about how electric and magnetic activity can be measured in the brain
- Have gained knowledge of neuroimaging techniques and how they can help in understanding psychological processes
- Understand how genetic techniques can contribute to psychobiological research
- Have an overview of psychophysiological measurements in the peripheral nervous system
- Have a basic understanding of neurostimulation techniques

DOI: 10.4324/9781003571537-8

Chapter 6

Learning from lesions

How studying the damaged brain can shed light on brain–behaviour associations

Introduction

The importance of investigating **brain lesions**, which are areas of brain tissue that have been damaged or destroyed by injury or illness, in the study of the brain and behaviour cannot be overstated. The basic idea is that we can gain insights into normal functioning by studying abnormal functioning. In a way, it can be thought of as reverse engineering: We attempt to understand the function of a brain region by observing what the person can and cannot do without it. Studying the lesioned brain enables us to establish direct links between specific regions of brain tissue and aspects of cognitive processing by carefully observing loss-of-function. As such, the field of **neuropsychology**, which investigates how brain injury or neurological disorders affect cognitive functions, plays a vital role in psychobiology.

The lesion method

The lesion method operates on a simple principle: if damage to a particular brain area impairs a specific mental function, that area is likely essential for that function. A key early link between damaged brain tissue and functional deficits was established by Pierre Paul Broca (1824–1880), a French neurologist, in the 1860s. Broca described a series of patients who were unable to produce speech but had otherwise normal intelligence. Post-mortem examinations revealed that

Brain lesions: A damaged or destroyed area of brain tissue. Lesions can happen due to injury or illness.

Neuropsychology: The branch of psychology that investigates how brain injury or neurological disorders affect cognitive functions.

DOI: 10.4324/9781003571537-9

Localisation of function: The concept that certain functions are situated in specific regions.

Broca's area: A region in the frontal lobe that is involved in speech production.

everyone had damage in roughly the same region: the posterior part of the left inferior frontal gyrus (IFG; see Figure 6.1). Broca therefore concluded that speech must be localised in the left hemisphere of the brain. These findings helped popularise the concept of **localisation of function**: specific brain regions are responsible for particular mental functions. This idea has been fundamental to neuropsychology and clinical neurology, even though we now also recognise that brain areas do not work entirely in isolation but also function as part of networks (see Chapter 5).

Broca's discoveries were so influential that the approximate region in the left IFG has become known as **Broca's area**. A few years later, German neurologist Carl Wernicke (1848–1905) reported a complementary finding: damage to an area in the upper left temporal lobe, now

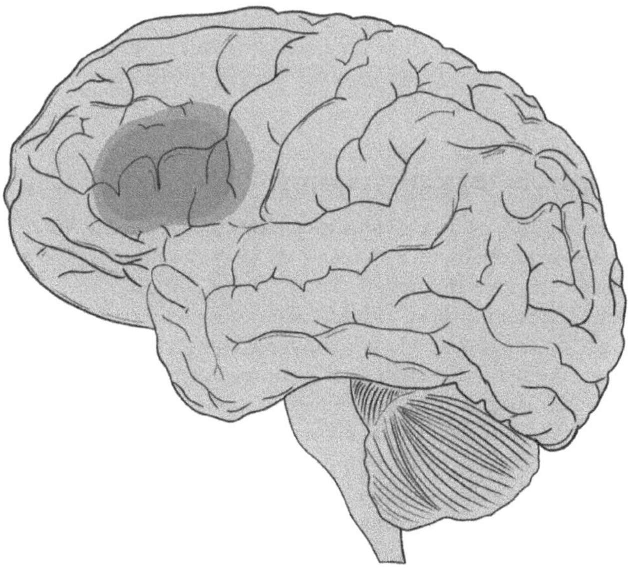

Figure 6.1 An image showing the left side of the brain, highlighting in red the frontal lobe area where Pierre Paul Broca (1824–1880) found damage responsible for speech loss, now known as Broca's area.

called **Wernicke's area**, caused problems with language comprehension. It resulted in fluent, but often unintelligible, speech. The term **aphasia** describes impairments in language comprehension and/or production caused by brain damage. People with **non-fluent aphasia (Broca's aphasia)** struggle with language production, while those with **fluent aphasia (Wernicke's aphasia)** can produce fluent but often meaningless speech and experience difficulties with language comprehension. The lesion method for studying brain–behaviour relationships experienced rapid growth after World War I and II, as many soldiers sustained damage to isolated brain regions due to gunshot injuries that clinicians could link to behaviour. These initial studies form the foundation of our current knowledge about how the brain underlies behaviour.

Wernicke's area: A region in the temporal lobe responsible for language comprehension.

Aphasia: Impairments in language comprehension and/or production caused by brain damage.

Non-fluent (Broca's) aphasia: Impairments with language production.

Fluent (Wernicke's) aphasia: Impairment characterised by fluent, meaningless speech and little language comprehension.

Neuropsychological assessment

Scientists often perform extensive psychological testing on patients who have suffered brain damage. This is very important to identify the exact nature of the deficit. For example, consider the many reasons someone might have trouble naming a picture of a penguin. It could be that the visual system is damaged and therefore cannot see the image. It might be that the visual form cannot be recognised because it cannot be matched to stored representations, or perhaps they recognise the object but cannot retrieve any information about it, including the name. Therefore, pinpointing the precise deficit is crucial and is performed using neuropsychological assessments, tests that determine which cognitive and behavioural abilities (such as pointing, lifting an arm, or emotional responses) are intact and which are impaired. There are many different neuropsychological test batteries (series of tests), and the choice of test performed can depend on the injury and other factors.

Dissociations in symptoms

One challenge in studying brain damage is that scientists cannot control the extent of the damage, except through participant selection. For example, a large lesion may affect multiple brain structures, making it difficult to identify which damaged area is responsible for a behavioural deficit. A non-invasive alternative, similar to the lesion method in some ways, involves using transcranial magnetic stimulation to create "virtual lesions", as explained further in Chapter 11. Another approach is to examine functional dissociations. If the same patient shows impairment on one task (task A) but not on another (task B), this is called a **single dissociation**. It may suggest that the tasks rely on different neural resources. However, it could also mean both tasks depend on the same neural resources, but to different extents. For instance, if task A depends more heavily on that resource and the lesion reduces it, then task A may be relatively more affected. An effective way to dismiss this resource-dependent possibility is to document a **double dissociation**. A double dissociation is demonstrated when two separate cases show opposite patterns of difficulty, indicating that each cognitive function can be disrupted without affecting the other and therefore operates independently. An interesting case is Pierrette Sapey (P.S.), who was hit by a London bus on Tower Bridge, suffering extensive brain damage in the right temporal and occipital lobes (Rossion, 2022). After her injury, P.S. lost the ability to recognise people's faces, including her own, but has no issues identifying other objects, fruits, vegetables, or even animals. Instead, she must rely on other cues, such as voice, posture, and clothing, to identify people. P.S. has what is called **prosopagnosia**, the selective inability to recognise faces following brain damage. Prosopagnosia is most often caused by right-sided or bilateral damage to the fusiform gyrus. In contrast, patient C.K. sustained a head injury in a motor vehicle accident while out jogging (Moscovitch et al., 1997). After the injury, C.K. was unable to recognise

Single dissociation: When a single patient is impaired on a particular task (task A) but spared on another task (task B).

Double dissociation: Is established when two cases show opposite difficulties: one has trouble with task A but not B and the other with task B but not A.

Prosopagnosia: The selective inability to recognise face identity, despite otherwise normal vision.

different objects, a condition called **visual object agnosia,** which is often associated with lesions in bilateral occipitotemporal cortex. C.K. had no trouble recognising faces, suggesting that some areas of the brain are essential for face recognition but not for visual object recognition, and vice versa. Of course, some people experience issues with both face and object recognition following brain damage. Do associations between deficits diminish dissociations? Most scientists argue not necessarily. Other factors, such as proximity in the brain, can explain why two symptoms appear together, for example, if a stroke affects both areas.

Visual object agnosia: An inability to recognise objects, despite otherwise normal vision.

Disconnection syndromes: A deficit that is caused by damage to white matter pathways that connect different areas in the brain.

Conduction aphasia: The inability to repeat back words and phrases.

Arcuate fasciculus: White matter bundle that connects Broca's area and Wernicke's area.

Disconnection syndromes

Brain lesions typically occur in the grey matter, which consists of the cell bodies and dendrites of neurons, but they can also impact the white matter, consisting of the myelinated axons that connect different brain areas. When damage to the connections in the brain results in specific deficits, it is referred to as a **disconnection syndrome**. An example of this is **conduction aphasia**, where a person cannot repeat words or phrases just spoken. As you just learned, Broca's area is vital for speech production, and Wernicke's area is essential for understanding speech. These areas are connected by a white matter tract known as the **arcuate fasciculus**. Damage to this tract is believed to cause conduction aphasia, allowing the individual to understand and produce speech but preventing them from repeating recent speech, as they cannot transmit the information they just processed to the speech output system. Disconnection syndromes are explored using diffusion magnetic resonance imaging (Chapter 8) and functional connectivity analyses (Chapter 5), helping us understand how different parts of the brain communicate.

"Planned" lesions and split-brain studies

Another method that has offered detailed insights into the brain is the use of "planned" lesions. This technique involves neurosurgeons removing a specific portion of brain tissue, often due to severe epilepsy that is unresponsive to medication or other treatments. Because these lesions are created surgically, the tissue is precisely removed, and cognitive performance can be compared before and after surgery, giving precise data on how different functions are impacted by the lesion. One of the most famous studied cases is H.M., which you can read about in Chapter 12.

Another example of surgical intervention, and arguably the most striking case for examining the effects of disconnection between brain regions, is split-brain research. These studies focus on individuals who have undergone a **corpus callosotomy**, a surgical operation that cuts the corpus callosum, the main connection between the two cerebral hemispheres. This procedure essentially divides the brain into two separate halves. In the 1960s and 1970s, Roger Sperry (1913–1994) and Michael Gazzaniga (1939-) conducted pioneering research with these patients, demonstrating that even when the hemispheres are disconnected, they can still process information independently. They also showed that the two hemispheres can perform slightly different functions, a phenomenon known as hemispheric specialisation.

Single-case studies versus group studies

Scientists use the lesion method through both single-case and group studies of people with brain lesions. **Single-case studies** involve detailed examinations of one individual, providing rich information about the nature of the damage and the cognitive profiles involved. They also allow for extensive follow-up of symptoms and recovery, offering detailed and precise data. However, it can be difficult to determine whether these findings will generalise to others. Therefore, scientists also conduct **group studies**, where groups of people with similar lesions (e.g., lesions in similar areas) or similar deficits (e.g., people

Corpus callosotomy: A surgical operation that cuts the corpus callosum, the main connection between the two cerebral hemispheres.

Single-case studies: The detailed examinations of one individual.

with related issues) are studied together. However, group studies can be challenging because many variables may differ between participants, not only the size and location of the lesion but also factors such as age, education levels, social environment, and other life experiences before and after the injury. Sometimes, scientists adopt a **multiple-case-study approach**, in which each individual's specific results are considered and compared across cases to explore similarities and differences.

> **Group studies**: Studies where groups of people with similar lesions (e.g., lesions in similar areas) or similar deficits (e.g., people with related issues) are studied.
>
> **Multiple-case-study approach**: A study in which everyone's specific results are considered and compared across cases to explore similarities and differences.
>
> **Voxel-level approach:** Methods that investigate the relationship between brain damage and behaviour at the level of individual voxels.

Lesion mapping using neuroimaging

The neuroanatomical investigation of lesions has been greatly facilitated by modern neuroimaging techniques such as magnetic resonance imaging, described in Chapter 8. These neuroimaging techniques provide very detailed images of people's brains, including the lesioned area(s), allowing careful mapping of the damage sustained. Lesion mapping is carried out for both single cases and for groups. As you remember, lesions are often quite large and variable in size. A basic group-level lesion comparison study takes individuals with a specific deficit (for example, working memory) and overlays images of each lesion on top of one another to identify areas of overlap, which are likely to contribute to the issue with working memory. The most commonly used method for lesion mapping is the **voxel-level approach** (Moore et al., 2024). This technique segments the brain into tiny 3D units called voxels, similar to pixels but in three dimensions. A statistical test is performed on each voxel to assess whether damage there can predict the associated deficit. Lesion mapping can also be performed for white matter tracts and for network-level connections.

Limitations of the lesion method

While the lesion method remains highly important in psychobiological research, it is essential to recognise its limitations. The most important point to remember is that we cannot directly observe the function performed by the damaged tissue; instead, we can only see how the rest of the brain functions without that area. We then infer the function of the lesioned tissue. Second, as mentioned earlier, multiple regions may work together and contribute to a specific function. If that function is disrupted, it only indicates that one brain region is critical for it, or perhaps that a vital connection between regions is damaged. It does not reveal the entire network of regions involved. We may also underestimate a region's importance if a person compensates by employing different strategies, such as using alternative brain regions to perform tasks, or through reorganisation (see Chapter 4). A brain region may be essential for a function, but after damage, the brain can reorganise so that the function is supported by a region that would not typically be involved. Lastly, brains do vary slightly across individuals in both structure and function depending on several factors, such as handedness, and these differences can also influence the behavioural effects of the lesion (explored in more detail in Chapter 17).

Conclusion

Lesion studies have laid the foundations for our current understanding of brain–behaviour relationships. By examining damaged brains, we can infer the functions of those regions in the normal brain. The study of damaged brains, combined with new technologies that enable highly precise, detailed examinations, will continue to advance psychobiological knowledge.

Further reading

Additional academic source: Kolb, B., & Whishaw, I. Q. (2021). *Fundamentals of Human Neuropsychology* (8th ed.). Macmillan.
Related book: Sacks, O. W. (2021). *The Man Who Mistook His Wife for a Hat and Other Clinical Tales.* Random House Inc.

References

Rossion, B. (2022). Twenty years of investigation with the case of prosopagnosia PS to understand human face identity recognition. Part I: function. *Neuropsychologia, 173*, 108278. https://doi.org/10.1016/j.neuropsychologia.2022.108278

Moore, M. J., Demeyere, N., Rorden, C., & Mattingley, J. B. (2024). Lesion mapping in neuropsychological research: a practical and conceptual guide. *Cortex, 170*, 38–52. https://doi.org/10.1016/j.cortex.2023.10.001

Moscovitch, M., Winocur, G., & Behrmann, M. (1997). What is special about face recognition? Nineteen experiments on a person with visual object agnosia and dyslexia but normal face recognition. *Journal of Cognitive Neuroscience, 9*(5), 555–604. https://doi.org/10.1162/jocn.1997.9.5.555

Chapter 7

Electric brains

The electroencephalogram in psychobiological research

Introduction

What are thoughts made of? From a psychobiological perspective, the answer to that question lies in activity in large networks of neurons. This activity is comprised of two major mechanisms: (1) the production of electric currents in the neuron, which propagate signals from cell bodies along axons and (2) chemical reactions in which neurotransmitters are released at the connections between the axon and other neurons. Psychobiological methods can assess both processes. In this chapter, we highlight two non-invasive key methodologies in psychobiology that measure the brain's electrical and magnetic activity.

Electroencephalogram

One of the most widely used methods in psychobiology is the **electroencephalogram (EEG),** which has been used for more than a hundred years (Mushtaq et al., 2024). Figure 7.1 shows a typical EEG recording scenario.

In an EEG recording session, the participating person wears an elastic cap over their head, which is fitted with electrodes (typical EEG setups include 32, 64, or 128 recording electrodes along with a reference electrode and a ground electrode, but other configurations are possible). The EEG signal (see Figure 7.1) is then recorded for each of these electrodes while the person performs a psychological task (task-based EEG), rests while awake (resting-state EEG), or sleeps (sleep EEG). The

Electroencephalogram (EEG): A psychobiological method that uses electrodes to record electrical activity on the scalp of the head to estimate electrical activity in the cortex of the brain.

DOI: 10.4324/9781003571537-10

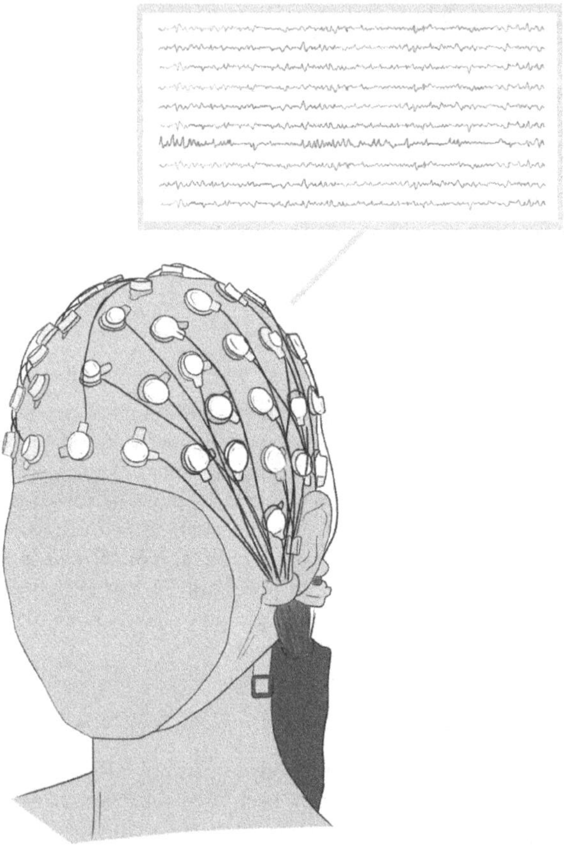

Figure 7.1 An EEG recording. The lower part of the figure shows a person wearing the typical EEG cap on which several EEG electrodes are fixated. The upper part of the figure shows the raw EEG signal measured from a number of these electrodes.

electrodes placed in the cap are connected to the person's scalp using a conductive EEG gel with a consistency similar to hair styling gel. They record the electrical activity on the scalp, which reflects the electrical activity of the brain. Since each neuron produces only a very small amount of electric energy, it is not possible to measure the activity of single neurons with an EEG. Instead, the recorded signal reflects the synchronised electric activity of larger clusters of neurons in the cortex. Since this signal is still rather weak, the EEG electrodes are connected to an amplifier, which in turn is connected to a computer running the EEG recording software.

Insights about electric brain activity can then be obtained by comparing changes in electric activity over time at different electrode sites in comparison to the reference electrode.

Compared to neuroimaging methods (see Chapter 9), the main drawback of EEG is its lower spatial resolution (it is difficult to pinpoint EEG activity to specific brain areas with high accuracy since the signal is recorded on the scalp). However, the major advantages are that EEG is much cheaper than most neuroimaging methods and has a much better temporal resolution (the EEG signal can be recorded in the millisecond range). It is completely non-invasive and can be performed with people of all ages, even infants. In medicine, EEG plays a major role in detecting epilepsy, sleep disorders, and determining the state of consciousness of a person. In psychobiological research, scientists typically focus on assessing normal brain function. To this end, they have developed two major ways to analyse the raw EEG signal.

Analysis of EEG frequency bands

One of the ways to analyse the raw EEG signal is the analysis of the different **EEG frequency bands**, sometimes also called brain waves or neural oscillations (Pascucci et al., 2025). These brain waves are rhythmic patterns in the EEG signal that occur at different frequencies. Figure 7.2 shows an example raw EEG signal and how it can be differentiated into the five most common EEG frequency bands. Table 7.1 shows the frequency range and functional relevance of these brain waves.

To determine EEG frequency bands in an EEG dataset, the raw EEG signal is first pre-processed (for example, cleaned of artefacts and noise due to eye movements or heartbeat in the data). The raw EEG is generally a mixture of the different frequency bands. Thus, it is not possible to directly observe the alpha band only by examining the raw signal. To obtain the different frequency bands, a so-called spectral decomposition of the raw EEG signal is performed. Analysis of different EEG frequency bands is central in psychobiological sleep research as it allows for an objective measure of conscious states. Using EEG, the different sleep phases can be determined objectively. It is also common in research on attention, memory, and cognition, as well as in clinical neuroscience.

EEG frequency bands: A way to analyse the raw EEG signal. The raw EEG signal is deconstructed into different frequency bands that have been related to different states of consciousness and cognition.

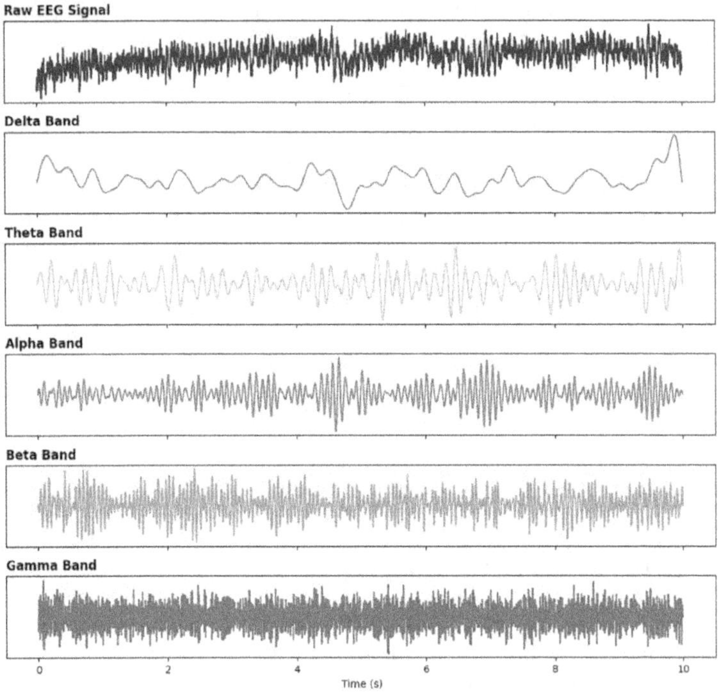

Figure 7.2 The raw EEG signal can be differentiated into several different frequency bands, including the delta, theta, alpha, beta, and gamma bands.

Table 7.1 The Five Major EEG Frequency Bands and Their Associated Functions

Frequency band name	*Frequency range*	*Functional relevance*
Delta band	Below 4 Hz	Person sleeps
Theta band	4–7 Hz	Person is drowsy
Alpha band	8–12 Hz	Person is relaxed but awake
Beta band	13–30 Hz	Person is actively thinking and concentrated
Gamma band	Above 30 Hz	Relevant for attention, memory, and conscious perception

Event-related potential (ERP): A way to analyse the raw EEG signal. ERPs are stereotypical patterns in the averaged EEG signal that can be identified after a certain event, such as the presentation of a stimulus or a response happened in the task.

Event-related potentials

In addition to analysing different frequency bands, a second widely used method of processing the raw EEG signal is to create so-called **event-related potentials (ERPs)** (Pütz et al., 2025). While the different EEG frequencies can be recorded during a task, at rest, or at sleep, ERPs are typically recorded during a psychological task. ERPs, as the name implies, are typical patterns in the EEG signal that can be identified after a certain event in a task. At the most general level, this event can be either the presentation of a stimulus (e.g., a visual stimulus such as a picture on a computer monitor or an auditory stimulus such as a spoken word presented over headphones) or a response by the person (such as pressing a button in response to seeing a picture). Because the EEG is recorded on the scalp, the signal generated in the brain is relatively small, and the data are generally noisy. Therefore, it is not possible to record an ERP with a single task trial. Instead, ERP tasks typically include several dozen or even hundreds of trials, which are averaged after the EEG signal has been pre-processed to clean it of noise in the data. Figure 7.3 shows a typical ERP figure. Table 7.2 shows examples of some commonly investigated ERPs in the psychobiological literature.

Mobile EEG

The classic EEG has one major drawback: because the amplifiers are large and the fact that the EEG electrodes, amplifier, and recording computer are connected by cables, it can typically only be recorded in laboratory environments and has low portability. Scientists in psychobiology often prefer laboratory environments for many studies as they are highly controllable, and many factors that could disturb data collection can be avoided. However, there are specific research questions for which data collection in the field is preferable, for example, when ecological validity (e.g., how well the results of a study reflect what happens in real life) and real-world application are in focus. Therefore, **mobile EEG (mEEG)** systems have been developed, which usually have much smaller amplifiers, which makes them portable and can be transported to the participants. They are also often wirelessly connected to the recording computer, or in some cases, record data on a smartphone or tablet.

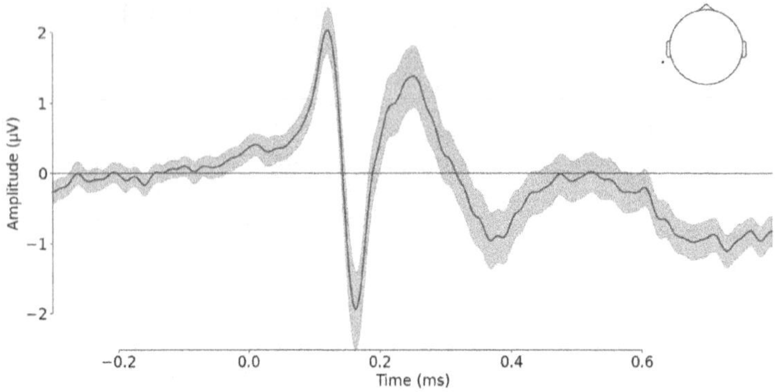

Figure 7.3 An example of a typical ERP component, obtained by averaging the EEG signal over many experimental trials in relation to a visual stimulus. The y-axis shows the amplitude of the averaged EEG signal in mV (micro volt). The x-axis shows the time in ms, with 0 indicating the time of the stimulus presentation (in this study, a word was presented on a computer screen). The solid blue line shows the average EEG signal, while the lighter blue area surrounding it indicates the confidence interval of the data surrounding the mean. There are many different ERP components that can be assessed using specific psychological tasks. Many, but not all of them, are named in a typical pattern in which a letter (either "P" for "positive" or "N" for "negative") is followed by a number, such as 1,2, 3. For example, the visual N1 ERP is the first negative peak after the presentation of a visual stimulus (such as a word shown on a computer screen) and occurs around 150 ms to 200 ms after the stimulus has been shown. Typically, the first part of ERP up to 200 ms reflects sensory processing of visual or auditory features, and the later part of the ERP reflects the 'thinking' part of the task.

Table 7.2 Examples of Common ERPs that Can Be Derived from the Raw EEG Signal and Their Associated Functions

ERP name	*Polarity and time range*	*Functional relevance*
Visual N1	Negative, 100 ms to 150 ms after a visual stimulus	Reflects selective attention
ERN (error-related negativity)	Negative, 80 ms to 150 ms after an incorrect motor response	Is observed when participants commit errors
N400	Negative, about 400 ms after a word has been seen or heard	Reflects word processing
P300	Positive, about 250 ms to 500 ms after a stimulus has been presented	Reflects stimulus evaluation
Late positive component	Positive, starting about 400 ms after stimulus presentation	Relevant for different forms of memory

Mobile EEG (mEEG): A small and portable EEG system that connects wirelessly to the recording device and allows for recording EEG data in many situations in which that was not possible with classic EEG.

They are also typically fitted with sensors that record 3-dimensional movement data of the head so that scientists can factor in movements in their analyses. mEEG has significantly increased the number of research questions that can be assessed with EEG. This is important for research areas in which real-life movements are highly relevant. For example, many classic EEG studies on emotional processing have people watch emotionally positive, negative, or neutral photos on a computer screen while the EEG signal is being recorded. However, this setup captures little of what it is like to experience emotions in real life. In contrast, an mEEG study on emotions towards one's partner had people hug, kiss, or read their partner a heartfelt love letter while EEG was recorded, which is a more realistic paradigm for understanding emotions in real life (Packheiser et al., 2021). mEEG has also revolutionised psychobiological research on the motor system. Many activities that could not be investigated in classic EEG research now can be studied, ranging from walking and playing basketball to bungee jumping or even swimming (Klapprott & Debener, 2024).

Intercranial EEG

While EEG and mEEG are recorded on the scalp, there is also a specific form of EEG in which the electrodes are placed directly in the brain, called intercranial EEG (iEEG). Since this is a highly invasive procedure that can only be performed in patients in whom the skull needs to be opened for medical reasons (e.g., due to brain surgery), it happens very rarely and only in a few people. iEEG is mainly used in the preparation of brain surgery related to epilepsy treatment to identify brain areas that may generate epileptic seizures. In recent years, it has also been discussed to what extent iEEG can be used in brain–computer interfaces to allow the control of computers using brain-derived signals. It will be exciting to see the developments in this field in the future.

Magnetoencephalography

A psychobiological technique that is closely related to the EEG is the magnetoencephalogram (MEG). In MEG, the electric currents produced by the brain are not directly measured using electrodes like in EEG.

Instead, the magnetic fields produced by this electric activity are measured by so-called magnetometers, devices that measure the magnetic field. Therefore, participants in MEG research do not wear an electrode cap like in EEG but sit under a tube-like machine that covers the upper part of their heads. Like EEG, MEG has the advantage over neuroimaging that it has a high temporal resolution and can record data in the millisecond range. Similar to EEG, it is used in research on perception and cognition, but is generally less common than EEG.

Magnetoencephalogram (MEG): A psychobiological method that records the magnetic field on the scalp of the head caused by activity in the cortex of the brain.

Conclusion

EEG is, without a doubt, one of the key methodologies in psychobiological research. With a history of over 100 years, it remains widely used, and in many research settings that lack access to more expensive neuroimaging methods, it is often the method of choice. Thanks to exciting new developments like mobile EEG, it will likely be a workhorse technique in psychology for years to come.

Further reading

Additional academic source: Borck, C. (2018). *Brainwaves: A Cultural History of Electroencephalography*. Routledge.

Additional academic source: Luck, S. J. (2014). *An Introduction to the Event-Related Potential Technique* (2nd ed.). The MIT Press.

Additional academic source: Perry, G. (2023). *Working with MEG. A Practical Guide to Magnetoencephalography*. Routledge.

Relevant web resource: https://www.eegmanylabs.org, the website of #EEGManyLabs, a large-scale, international replication effort in which scientists recreated influential EEG experiments.

References

Klapprott, M., & Debener, S. (2024). Mobile EEG for the study of cognitive-motor interference during swimming? *Frontiers in Human Neuroscience, 18*, 1466853. https://doi.org/10.3389/fnhum.2024.1466853

Mushtaq, F., Welke, D., Gallagher, A., Pavlov, Y. G., Kouara, L., Bosch-Bayard, J., van den Bosch, J. J. F., Arvaneh, M., Bland, A. R., Chaumon, M., Borck, C., He, X., Luck, S. J., Machizawa, M. G., Pernet, C., Puce, A., Segalowitz, S. J.,

Rogers, C., Awais, M., ... Valdes-Sosa, P. (2024). One hundred years of EEG for brain and behaviour research. *Nature Human Behaviour, 8*, 1437–1443. https://doi.org/10.1038/s41562-024-01941-5

Packheiser, J., Berretz, G., Rook, N., Bahr, C., Schockenhoff, L., Güntürkün, O., & Ocklenburg, S. (2021). Investigating real-life emotions in romantic couples: a mobile EEG study. *Scientific Reports, 11*, 1142. https://doi.org/10.1038/s41598-020-80590-w

Pascucci, D., Menétrey, M. Q., Passarotto, E., Luo, J., Paramento, M., & Rubega, M. (2025). EEG brain waves and alpha rhythms: past, current and future direction. *Neuroscience and Biobehavioral Reviews, 176*, 106288. Advance online publication. https://doi.org/10.1016/j.neubiorev.2025.106288

Pütz, C., Span, M., & Lorist, M. (2025). Protocol for designing, conducting, and analyzing event-related potentials in human participants. *STAR Protocols, 6*, 103835. https://doi.org/10.1016/j.xpro.2025.103835

Chapter 8

A colourful revolution

Neuroimaging and its relevance for psychobiology

Introduction

Charlie had heard about magnetic resonance imaging (MRI) scans before, mostly for brain research. Today, they were about to undergo one as part of a study on language lateralisation. They were both curious and nervous. The staff at the research centre greeted them friendly. Charlie was asked to fill out some forms, including questions about health and metal implants. After all, MRI scanners use a strong magnetic field, so it is important to ensure there's no interference from metal. The technician explained that they would need to lie very still while the machine took detailed images of their brain. Earplugs were provided to block the loud scanner noise, and a coil was placed around their head to capture signals from the brain (see Figure 8.1). Charlie was asked to perform simple language tasks, such as thinking of words or evaluating sentences. The scan was loud, but Charlie focused on staying calm and still. The experiment ended after an hour, and the technician helped them out of the scanner. Charlie felt proud to have contributed to important psychobiological research.

Neuroimaging techniques have revolutionised our understanding of the brain and its related behaviours. While we once depended on post-mortem examinations and invasive methods, we can now visualise structures and processes in the living human brain. Techniques like MRI provide high spatial resolution of brain structures. These methods continue to develop, enabling detailed studies of the brain. They have provided us with a much deeper understanding of both human and animal brains. In this chapter, we present some of the key neuroimaging methods in psychobiology.

Computed tomography

Computed tomography (CT) is a structural imaging method that uses X-rays to produce detailed three-dimensional images of the brain. It is

DOI: 10.4324/9781003571537-11

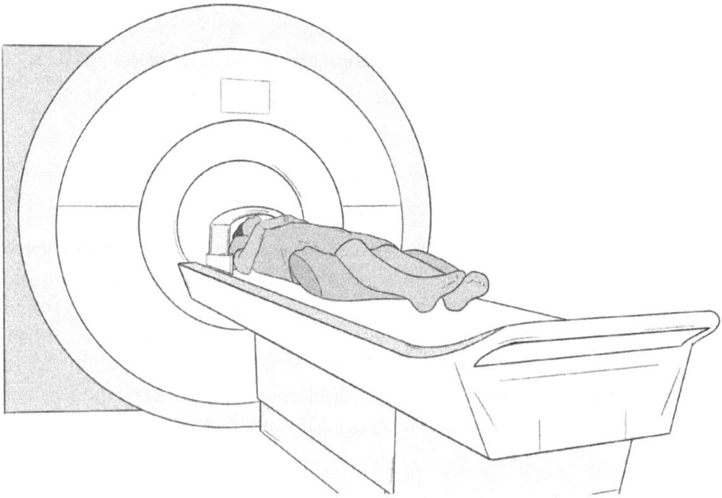

Figure 8.1 A person lying down and preparing to enter the MRI scanner. The head is positioned inside a helmet-like device called a head coil, which detects signals from the brain used to create detailed images.

> **Computed tomography (CT):** A structural imaging method that uses X-rays to produce detailed three-dimensional images of the brain.

based on the principle that different tissue types, such as bone, grey matter, white matter, and cerebrospinal fluid (CSF), have unique physical properties. X-ray absorption depends on tissue density: bone absorbs the most, making the skull appear white in images; CSF absorbs the least and appears very dark; grey matter falls in between and appears grey. A typical brain CT scan is quick, often taking only a few minutes. Since CT scans involve X-ray exposure, the person undergoing the scan receives a small amount of radiation. For this reason, CT is mainly used in clinical practice and is less common in research. In medicine, for example, CT helps identify brain bleeds, major structural abnormalities, or bone damage. Compared to MRI, CT provides less detail of soft tissues.

Magnetic resonance imaging

The most widely used and probably the most powerful imaging method in psychobiology is **MRI**. Its strength comes from the fact that the magnetic

Magnetic resonance imaging (MRI): A non-invasive method that uses an MR scanner to produce detailed images of the inside of the body.

resonance (MR) scanner is a highly versatile tool because we can adjust its settings to examine different types of tissues inside the brain, including soft tissues such as grey matter and white matter, as well as provide information on how the brain functions. MRI scanners are commonly found in hospitals, making them highly accessible, and many universities now also have research-dedicated MRI scanners as part of their facilities. The technique is completely non-invasive, meaning no injections are performed, and it is safe, allowing people to be scanned multiple times. However, a limitation of the technique is that not everyone can undergo a scan in the MRI machine for various reasons: people with metal implants or pacemakers may not be able to undergo MRI scans safely, as the strong magnetic field can cause the implants to move, heat up or interfere with electronic devices. Some people also become claustrophobic in the scanner, as it involves spending a long time in a narrow space. In addition, MRI scanners are expensive to maintain and operate, which means they are not accessible to everyone.

Structural MRI

MRI scans can provide very detailed information about brain anatomy. The cylindrical tube of the MR scanner shown in Figure 8.1 contains a powerful electromagnet that generates a constant magnetic field. The strength of the magnet is measured in units called Tesla (T), and most research scanners have a field strength of 3T, which is about 50,000 times stronger than Earth's magnetic field. The human body contains many hydrogen atoms, mostly in water and fat, and it is the protons (the nuclei of hydrogen atoms) that produce the MRI signal. These protons have weak magnetic fields and have a property called spin, which gives them a magnetic orientation. Normally, these spins are randomly oriented, but when placed in the strong magnetic field of the MRI, they tend to align either with or against it. When a pulse of radio waves (RF pulse) is applied at an appropriate frequency, it can change the orientation of the spins as the protons absorb energy. After the radio waves are turned off, the protons relax back to their original orientations with the magnetic field, releasing the absorbed energy as radio signals. These signals are detected and used to generate detailed images of the brain's internal structures, as different tissue types contain varying amounts of water and respond slightly differently when stimulated, resulting in different image intensities. For example, in a T1-weighted image, grey matter appears grey, white matter appears white, and CSF appears very dark, as can be seen in Figure 8.2. This technique can be used to produce detailed images of grey matter (see Chapter 2) in the brain.

Diffusion-weighted imaging

The MR machine can also be used to visualise white matter in the brain. However, the T1-weighted images described above only show overall structure (anatomy) and do not easily reveal the finer details of different white matter tracts. Instead, **diffusion-weighted imaging (DWI)** is the preferred method for studying fine details in white matter, seen in Figure 8.2. DWI detects the movement of water molecules within brain tissue, allowing to identify subtle microstructural changes that are not visible on standard brain scans. Within liquid-filled spaces like the ventricles in the brain, water molecules have to same chance to move freely in each direction. However, within white matter tracts, water molecules are more likely to move along the direction of the tract than in other directions. This principle enables DWI to map the orientation and integrity of white matter tracts. A common method for examining white matter structure is called **diffusion tensor imaging (DTI).**

Diffusion weighted imaging (DWI): detects water-molecule movement within brain tissue, enabling the identification of subtle microstructural properties of the brain.

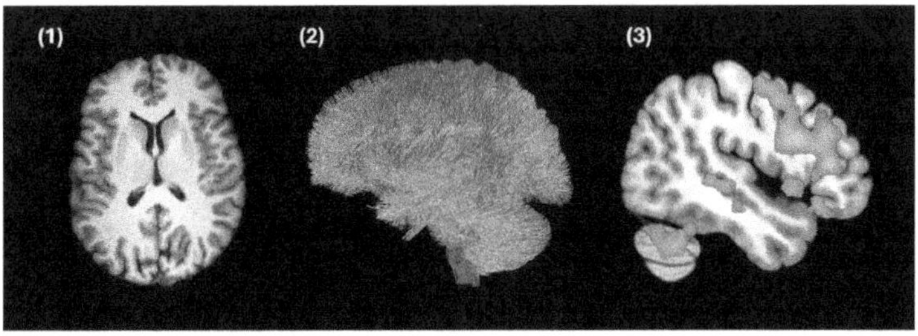

Figure 8.2 Three examples of different brain images: (1) a T1-weighted structural image; (2) a diffusion-weighted image showing white matter pathways, colour-coded by direction (red: right to left, green: anterior to posterior, blue: superior to inferior); and (3) task-based fMRI activation.

A relatively new DWI technique, **neurite orientation dispersion and density imaging (NODDI)**, was developed to examine the microstructure of axons and dendrites (known collectively as neurites) in the brain (Zhang et al., 2012). As you will remember from Chapter 3, neurites are projections of neurons. The technique allows measurements of both neurite density, using the neurite density index, and orientation dispersion, using the orientation dispersionindex. Thus, NODDI is useful when you are interested in overall tissue microstructure.

Diffusion tensor imaging (DTI): A type of DWI that examines brain white matter pathways by measuring water-molecule diffusion.

Neurite orientation dispersion and density imaging (NODDI): An imaging technique to examine the microstructure of axons and dendrites.

Functional magnetic resonance imaging (fMRI): A functional imaging technique that uses the MR scanner to measure changes in the BOLD signal as an indirect marker of neural activity.

Blood oxygen-level-dependent (BOLD) signal: The signal measured in fMRI that reflects local changes in the concentration of deoxygenated haemoglobin, which occur in response to neuronal activity and associated changes in blood flow.

Functional MRI

While structural imaging creates static images of the brain (brain anatomy), **functional magnetic resonance imaging (fMRI)** measures the brain in action (Soares, et al., 2016). It does this indirectly by assuming that changes in oxygenated (oxygen-rich) and deoxygenated (oxygen-poor) blood reflect neural activity. When neurons are active, they use oxygen supplied by red blood cells. Therefore, when an area is active, it receives an increased supply of oxygen-rich blood. fMRI measures the **blood oxygen-level-dependent (BOLD)** contrast, which reflects local changes in the concentration of deoxygenated haemoglobin since this can be detected by the MR scanner. Importantly, fMRI does not measure absolute levels of brain activity but rather relative changes in blood oxygenation over time. This comparison is performed for every single voxel, which is the 3D equivalent of a 2D pixel. Voxels usually range from 1 to 3 mm^3 in size, which is why fMRI has excellent spatial resolution. As blood flow changes occur more slowly than neural activity, fMRI has a relatively limited temporal resolution, measuring changes over seconds

Task-based fMRI: A form of fMRI that measures brain activity as a person performs a specific task, enabling researchers to identify the involved brain regions.

Resting-state fMRI: A form of fMRI that captures brain activity while the individual is at rest and not engaged in any task. This approach allows researchers to study the brain's spontaneous activity and to identify functional connections between regions.

rather than milliseconds, as in EEG.

During a scan, a series of brain images is captured over time, enabling researchers to study how brain activity varies. There are different types of fMRI scans, with **task-based fMRI** being the most common. In such studies, participants perform specific tasks inside the scanner, like thinking of words or viewing images of faces. The BOLD contrast is then compared with a rest or "control" condition, in which participants perform similar activities that do not involve the targeted cognitive function. The scientists then use complex statistical models to identify brain regions with consistent changes in the BOLD signal across the conditions. These changes are typically expressed as colourful images, as shown in Figure 8.2. Another type of fMRI scan is **resting-state fMRI**, which is conducted while a person is resting. It measures spontaneous fluctuations in the BOLD signal to examine functional networks in the brain (see Chapter 5).

fMRI provides the most detailed non-invasive way to study brain activity, making it a key tool in psychobiological research. Despite its advantages, it is costly and complex, and since it measures blood flow rather than directly capturing neuronal activity, interpreting its findings requires careful analysis and large, well-structured studies. Fortunately, large-scale initiatives such as the Human Connectome Project and UK Biobank, along with multi-lab collaborations, now enable the study of brain function across large and diverse populations.

Positron emission tomography

Positron emission tomography (PET) is another technique that creates 3D images of the inside of the body by using a small amount of radioactive material to monitor changes in metabolism and blood flow (Lameka, et al., 2016). Usually injected into the bloodstream or ingested, the **radioactive tracer** accumulates in specific areas depending on its type. When it reaches these areas, it emits **positrons**, which are positively charged particles with the same mass and charge magnitude as electrons. These positrons interact with electrons, producing pairs of gamma rays that are detected by the PET scanner. The most common radioactive tracer in PET scans is fluorodeoxyglucose (^{18}F-FDG), a glucose analogue that accumulates in tissues with high energy demands, such as the brain. Various other tracers have been developed, including those targeting brain chemicals such as dopamine and serotonin. Although the technique was initially used for brain research, this role has largely been taken over by fMRI, which does not require the injection of radioactive tracers. PET is now increasingly used in clinical settings. For example, in oncology, PET helps detect cancers because many tumours show increased metabolic activity compared to normal tissue. It can also detect β-amyloid plaques associated with Alzheimer's disease.

Positron emission tomography (PET): A functional imaging technique that produces images by using a small amount of radioactive material to monitor changes in metabolism and blood flow.

Radioactive tracer: A small quantity of radioactive material administered into the body to monitor the movement of organs, tissues, or chemicals, and is visible through specialised imaging scans, like PET.

Positron: A positively charged subatomic particle that has the same mass and magnitude of charge as an electron.

Functional near-infrared spectroscopy

Functional near-infrared spectroscopy (fNIRS) is a brain imaging method that detects brain activity by monitoring changes in blood oxygen levels, similar to fMRI. Unlike fMRI, fNIRS uses safe near-infrared light that can penetrate the skin and skull to measure blood oxygen levels. Molecules in oxygenated and deoxygenated haemoglobin absorb light differently, allowing them to be distinguished. The fNIRS device consists of two types of sensors, called optodes: a transmitter that emits light into the head and a receiver that detects the scattered light returning to the scalp. By analysing the absorption of light at various wavelengths, it's possible to estimate the amounts of oxygenated and deoxygenated haemoglobin in specific regions. Since the reflected signal is relative, it must be compared to a baseline measurement of the same region taken during rest.

Functional near-infrared spectroscopy (fNIRS): A functional imaging technique that uses near-infrared light to measure blood oxygen levels.

Functional transcranial Doppler sonography (fTCD): A functional imaging technique that uses ultrasound to measure blood flow velocity in the brain.

fNIRS systems vary in size and complexity. Smaller models, typically with around eight channels and resembling lightweight headbands, mainly measure activity in the prefrontal cortex. Medium-sized systems with 16–18 channels offer wider coverage of frontal and temporal areas while remaining portable. Larger, research-grade systems use caps similar to EEG caps and can cover most of the cortex with over 128 channels. Although fNIRS is easy to operate, one drawback is that it only measures activation in the cortex and cannot detect activity in deeper brain structures. It is also limited to a spatial resolution of 2–3 cm. Nonetheless, the main advantages of fNIRS are that it is much cheaper than fMRI, very resistant to motion artefacts, and that newer setups are becoming lighter and more portable, including wireless systems (Pinti et al., 2020). It is also worth noting that NIRS recording is silent, relatively comfortable, and imposes no physical constraints on participants, making it well-suited for use with infants, auditory studies, and studies involving movement.

Functional transcranial Doppler sonography

Functional transcranial Doppler sonography (fTCD) is a neurophysiological imaging tool used to measure blood flow velocity in the brain's major arteries during cognitive tasks. It works by projecting low-frequency ultrasound waves through the temporal bone window, an area in front of the ear where the skull is thin enough for the waves to reach the brain's blood vessels. Blood flow velocity is determined by measuring the frequency change between transmitted and reflected ultrasound waves caused by moving blood cells, a phenomenon known as the Doppler effect. Like fMRI and fNIRS, changes in cerebral blood flow velocity are believed to reflect increased energy demands as brain cells become more active, making it an indirect measure of brain activity. The primary advantage of fTCD is that it is inexpensive and easy to use compared to fMRI and PET. It is also more resistant to head movements, portable, and suitable for populations that are difficult to scan, such as young children. However, fTCD has limited spatial resolution, which depends on the size of the cortical areas supplied by the artery under study, most often the middle cerebral artery that supplies blood to about 50% of the cortex. This means that brain activity cannot be localised precisely as in fMRI. The technique is primarily used to assess cerebral lateralisation of cognitive abilities by comparing task-related activation between the left and right cerebral hemispheres.

Conclusion

Neuroimaging techniques have revolutionised how we understand the brain and associated behaviours. They allow us to visualise different tissue types like grey matter and white matter, as well as observe the brain in action. As these methods advance, it will be exciting to see the increased detail possible in brain research in the upcoming decades.

Further reading

Additional academic source: de Beeck, H. O., & Nakatani, C. (2019). *Introduction to Human Neuroimaging*. Cambridge University Press.

Additional academic source: Westbrook, C. (2016). *MRI at a Glance* (3rd ed.). John Wiley & Sons.

References

Lameka, K., Farwell, M. D., & Ichise, M. (2016). Positron emission tomography. *Handbook of Clinical Neurology*, *135*, 209–227. https://doi.org/10.1016/B978-0-444-53485-9.00011-8

Pinti, P., Tachtsidis, I., Hamilton, A., Hirsch, J., Aichelburg, C., Gilbert, S., & Burgess, P. W. (2020). The present and future use of functional near-infrared spectroscopy (fNIRS) for cognitive neuroscience. *Annals of the New York Academy of Sciences, 1464*(1), 5–29. https://doi.org/10.1111/nyas.13948

Soares, J. M., Magalhães, R., Moreira, P. S., Sousa, A., Ganz, E., Sampaio, A., Alves, V., Marques, P., & Sousa, N. (2016). A Hitchhiker's guide to functional magnetic resonance imaging. *Frontiers in Neuroscience*, *10*, 515. https://doi.org/10.3389/fnins.2016.00515

Zhang, H., Schneider, T., Wheeler-Kingshott, C. A., & Alexander, D. C. (2012). NODDI: practical in vivo neurite orientation dispersion and density imaging of the human brain. *Neuroimage*, *61*(4), 1000–1016. https://doi.org/10.1016/j.neuroimage.2012.03.072

Chapter 9

What parents provide

Neurogenetics in psychobiology

Introduction

Psychology is deeply rooted in biology. While it is obvious that the neurobiology of the brain is highly relevant to most research questions in psychology, the relevance of biological mechanisms for psychology goes right to the molecular level.

In particular, genetic methods have had a major impact on psychobiological research since the human **genome** was fully sequenced in the early 2000s. The genome is the entirety of genetic information carried by the **deoxyribonucleic acid (DNA)** in a cell of an organism. A **gene** is a section of the DNA. Genes can be protein-coding or non-protein-coding. Genetics has revolutionised our understanding of both the pathogenesis of major mental health disorders, like depression or schizophrenia, and non-clinical traits in psychobiology. For example, a large Danish study by Hilker et al. (2018) found that schizophrenia has a heritability of 79%, indicating a substantial genetic influence on the risk of developing the disorder. Regarding non-clinical traits, intelligence is largely determined by genetic factors, with a heritability of 80%.

> **Genome**: The genome is the entirety of genetic information carried by the DNA in a cell of an organism.
>
> **Deoxyribonucleic acid (DNA)**: A large molecule that is organised as a double helix and carries the genetic information of an organism.
>
> **Gene**: A gene is a section of the DNA. Genes can be protein-coding or non-protein-coding.

Findings like these have fundamentally changed our understanding of both mental health disorders and the basics of human behaviour and cognition. For example, in the 1950s, a widely discussed theory on the emergence of autism was the now-refuted "refrigerator mother" theory,

DOI: 10.4324/9781003571537-12

which assumed that a child develops autism if their mother does not provide emotional warmth. Thus, it was thought that autism was caused by an environmental factor: the mother's lack of emotional warmth. The theory not only reinforced the prejudice that care work should be provided by women but also placed significant stress on mothers of autistic children, who may have been blamed for their child's condition by other family members. We now know that complex genetic factors and their interaction with environmental factors play a large role in autism. This shows how psychobiological research can help combat harmful gender stereotypes and support a more inclusive understanding of mental health and psychological functions.

Single-nucleotide polymorphisms: application in psychology and methodological issues

Psychobiological research has used several different genetic techniques that utilise specific molecular features of the human genome. DNA consists of two strands that form a double helix. The units that form these strands consist of one of four different bases abbreviated by a letter (C: cytosine, G: guanine, A: adenine, and T: thymine) and further components. A DNA strand can be imagined as a long sequence of these letters, like "GCAAAAAATTTGAGA" (but much longer). Almost all of the sequence DNA is identical between the genomes of different people. Remarkably, about 99.6% of letters are identical between any two people, and all genetic differences between them are due to 0.4% of the genome. Thus, you, dear reader, are approximately 99.6% genetically identical to famous stars like Taylor Swift or Harry Styles. Many early genetic studies in psychobiology in the 2000s and 2010s focused on the analyses of the 0.4% of the DNA that shows variations between individuals.

Specifically, these studies investigated so-called **single-nucleotide polymorphisms (SNPs)**. An SNP is a form of genetic variation that is present in at least 1% of the population and consists of a variation in a single base. Since everyone has two DNA strands, three different **genotypes** can emerge for each SNP (e.g., if there is

> **Single-nucleotide polymorphism (SNP)**: An SNP is a form of genetic variation that is present in at least 1% of the population and consists of a variation in a single base.
>
> **Genotype**: The genotype of a person for a specific gene is the specific variants of this gene that a person carries.

Phenotype: An observable trait of a person. In psychobiological research, relevant phenotypes are often whether someone shows a disorder like depression or the extent of a psychological trait such as a high or low intelligence quotient for intelligence.

Genome-wide association study (GWAS): A type of molecular genetic study in which two groups (e.g., patients and controls) are statistically compared regarding many genetic markers across the whole genome to identify genetic loci that are associated with the emergence of a disorder or psychological trait.

a C-to-T exchange, the three possible genotypes are CC, TT, and CT). By collecting DNA from participants using blood or saliva samples and then statistically comparing the three genotype groups for an SNP regarding a psychological **phenotype** (observable trait) such as depression or intelligence, one could find out whether the gene that contains the SNP may be relevant for the trait. For example, if a researcher finds that the three genotype groups defined by an SNP that is located within a serotonin transporter gene show differences in depression scores, it may be concluded that the gene may be relevant for depression. At the end of the 2010s, studies based on analysing SNPs came under heavy criticism in the psychobiological research community for two reasons. First, it became clear that the effects of genetic factors on mental health disorders or psychological functions were driven by complex networks of many genes and not variations in single genes. Many SNP studies, therefore, underestimated the real biological complexity of the investigated traits. Secondly, many SNP-based studies had low sample sizes that led to low statistical power and replication issues. This led to a paradigm shift in that psychobiological studies today focus more on genome-wide association studies (GWAS) described in the next section.

GWAS in psychobiology

The two main issues of studies that investigated single SNPs were remedied by an advanced technology based on SNPs, so-called **GWAS**. For a typical SNP-based study, researchers would identify a small number of SNPs that may be biologically relevant for a certain behaviour or disorder and then determine the individual genotype of the participants in their study. This, of course, has the risk that highly relevant SNPs may not be tested, as the researchers did not know about them. In GWAS, this problem is solved by comparing genetic markers for two groups across the whole genome (hence the name). Using so-called SNP arrays, researchers can assess variation in millions of SNPs across the genome. This reduces the risk of overlooking relevant variations but comes at a cost: Since a GWAS typically includes a vastly larger number of comparisons than a typical study in psychobiology, researchers must perform massive corrections for multiple comparisons to avoid a high number of false positive results due to alpha error inflation. In short, if you make many statistical comparisons, there will be some that give a positive result, despite there being no true difference between groups. If you make thousands or millions of statistical comparisons, naturally, there will be many such false positive results. Therefore, GWAS commonly assume a so-called genome-wide significance threshold of $p < 5 \times 10^{-8}$ ($p<0.000000005$) instead of $p < 0.05$ which is the significance threshold most often used in psychological research. To gain enough statistical power (the ability of a test to detect a difference that exists) to test effects at this level, GWAS typically include sample sizes much larger than those typically found in psychobiological studies. In some GWAS, the number of participants can exceed one million, a number that can only be acquired by large multinational research teams including several research institutes. GWASs have changed the way we understand the molecular underpinnings of mental health disorders and psychological traits, generally showing that these traits have a much more complex genetic architecture than thought based on previous research. For example, a GWAS on schizophrenia in more than 70,000 patients and more than 240,000 controls identified 287 distinct genomic loci associated with schizophrenia (Trubetskoy et al., 2022). For educational attainment, a common proxy for intelligence in psychobiological research, a study with about 3 million participants identified 3,952 genomic loci (Okbay et al., 2022). Different types of additional analyses can then be used to identify functional genetic pathways (e.g., groups of genes that together affect a biological function like the growth of neurons) relevant to the investigated traits. GWAS can also be used to the genetic factors underlying variation in different brain structures, giving rise to the research field of neurogenetics, an important emerging field of research in psychobiology.

Whole-exome sequencing: including rare variants

SNPs are often also called common variants as they are present in at least 1% of the population. They are, however, not the only form of genetic variants a person can show. In addition, there are so-called rare variants that are present in less than 1% of the population. Despite their rarity, they may be highly relevant in psychobiological research. It has been argued that some rare variants may have strong effects on brain and behaviour, since evolutionary

Exome: A small part of the genome (1.1%) that mostly consists of the parts of the DNA that code for proteins.

Gene expression: The process in which the information encoded in a gene is used to produce a protein or other gene product.

selection processes may keep particularly deleterious variants at low frequencies. For example, it has been shown that rare variants in the gene *FOXP1* are associated with severe language problems, autism features, and cognitive impairment. Investigations into *FOXP1* have led to important insights into the neurobiology of language that would not have been possible by only investigating common variants. Consequently, rare variants have been increasingly studied in psychobiology in recent years and can be investigated using a technique called whole-exome sequencing. The **exome** is a small part of the genome (1.1%) that mostly consists of the parts of the DNA that code for proteins. Thus, whole-exome sequencing focuses on the parts of the genome that may have a particularly strong effect on brain and behaviour, and it includes both common and rare variants in these genes. Using whole-exome sequencing, recent psychobiological studies could reveal rare variants relevant to sleep patterns, alcohol consumption, and depression – among many other things.

Gene expression analysis in psychobiology

In addition to whole-exome sequencing, another class of molecular genetic methods that have recently gained traction in psychobiological research includes techniques that do not focus on common or rare variants in the DNA itself, but on the gene products that affect the development of the organism. The process in which the information encoded in a gene is used to produce a protein or other gene product is called **gene expression**. Using gene expression analysis, the association between gene expression in cells from specific samples (such as blood or saliva) and mental health disorders or psychological traits can be assessed. Since gene expression is tissue-specific (e.g., it is different in brain tissue or blood) and the brain is the most relevant tissue for psychological processes, gene expression studies are often performed on post-mortem brain samples. Some studies also use blood samples from living people, but it is unclear to what extent these results are relevant to the brain. This way, it was shown that depression is associated with differential expression of genes related to inflammation, stress processing, neuroplasticity, and neurotransmitters (Mariani et al., 2021).

Gene–environment interactions and epigenetics

Genetic factors are not the only influences on mental health disorders and psychological traits. Early childhood adversity, such as parental neglect or violence against children, the social environment, pollutants and toxins in the physical environment, and drug use, are just a few examples of environmental factors that affect brain structure and function and ultimately impact psychological well-being and mental health.

Some of these environmental factors directly affect these functions, largely independent of genetic factors. For example, alcohol acts as a potent neurotoxin, and excessive drinking over time can cause neurotoxic effects that lead to alcohol-related brain damage. For many traits and disorders, however, so-called gene–environment interactions have been described. A gene–environment interaction means that the impact of an environmental factor, such as stress, on the development of a disorder or specific psychological trait depends on individual variations in a person's genome. For example, it has been shown that the effect of stressful life events on the risk of developing depression is moderated by the genotype. This means that for people with no stressful life events, the number of genetic risk factors does not affect their low probability of developing depression (Caspi et al., 2003). However, for people who experienced severely stressful life events, the risk of developing depression is decidedly higher for people who possess genetic risk factors for depression than for those who do not.

A key question in developmental psychobiology is how exactly environmental factors like early adversity in childhood or stress affect gene function on the molecular level. The biological mechanisms that underlie how environmental factors affect the expression of genes, and therefore their protein products, are investigated in the research field of epigenetics. Epigenetic processes can switch the expression of genes "on" or "off", but do not structurally change the DNA. For example, epigenetic processes in psychology have been investigated in the so-called Romanian orphan studies. When Romanian dictator Nicolae Ceauşescu was overthrown in the late 1980s, it was discovered that many thousand infants and children in Romanian orphanages had been severely neglected. These neglected children developed several different socio-emotional, language, and mental health issues. Analyses of DNA methylation, an epigenetic process that leads to a "switching off" of genes, in a sample of these children revealed that severe neglect in early life affected the DNA methylation of the gene *CYP2E1*, with elevated methylation being associated with stronger impairments in social cognition (Kumsta et al., 2016). In this way, the scientists could reveal a potential neurobiological mechanism that connects early adversity to social cognitive abilities.

Conclusion

Mental health disorders and psychological traits like intelligence are determined by complex interactions between genetic and environmental factors that can be investigated using the techniques described in this chapter. While more reminiscent of molecular biology than classical psychobiological research techniques, they have been proven indispensable for getting deeper insights into how and why people develop mental health disorders or show specific psychological phenotypes such as very high or low intelligence. These insights would have been impossible to obtain by using classic psychological research methods, showing how crucial multidisciplinary research is. As tremendous progress continues to be made in the development of molecular genetic methods, it is exciting to see how these developments will shape psychobiology. After all, each one of us will carry the genes our parents provided to us for the rest of our lives.

Further reading

Additional academic source: Knopik, V. S., Neiderhiser, J. M., DeFries, J. C., & Plomin, R. (2017). *Behavioral Genetics* (7th ed.). Worth Publishers Macmillan Learning.

Relevant web resource: The dataset of the UK biobank, the biggest while-genome dataset in the world, is used in many psychological studies: https://www.ukbiobank.ac.uk/about-our-data/types-of-data/genetic-data/

Related film: *Gattaca* (1997). A science fiction film focused on the topic of genetic discrimination.

References

Caspi, A., Sugden, K., Moffitt, T. E., Taylor, A., Craig, I. W., Harrington, H., McClay, J., Mill, J., Martin, J., Braithwaite, A., & Poulton, R. (2003). Influence of life stress on depression: moderation by a polymorphism in the 5-HTT gene. *Science, 301*, 386–389. https://doi.org/10.1126/science.1083968

Hilker, R., Helenius, D., Fagerlund, B., Skytthe, A., Christensen, K., Werge, T. M., Nordentoft, M., & Glenthøj, B. (2018). Heritability of schizophrenia and schizophrenia spectrum based on the nationwide Danish twin register. *Biological Psychiatry, 83*, 492–498. https://doi.org/10.1016/j.biopsych.2017.08.017

Kumsta, R., Marzi, S. J., Viana, J., Dempster, E. L., Crawford, B., Rutter, M., Mill, J., & Sonuga-Barke, E. J. S. (2016). Severe psychosocial deprivation in early childhood is associated with increased DNA methylation across a region spanning the transcription start site of CYP2E1. *Translational Psychiatry, 6*, e830. https://doi.org/10.1038/tp.2016.95

Mariani, N., Cattane, N., Pariante, C., & Cattaneo, A. (2021). Gene expression studies in Depression development and treatment: an overview of the underlying molecular mechanisms and biological processes to identify biomarkers. *Translational Psychiatry, 11*, 354. https://doi.org/10.1038/s41398-021-01469-6

Okbay, A., Wu, Y., Wang, N., Jayashankar, H., Bennett, M., Nehzati, S. M., Sidorenko, J., Kweon, H., Goldman, G., Gjorgjieva, T., Yunxuan, J., Hicks, B., Tian, C., Hinds, D. A., Ahlskog, R., Magnusson, P. K. E., Oskarsson, S., Hayward, C., Campbell, A., … Young, A. I. (2022). Polygenic prediction of educational attainment within and between families from genome-wide association analyses in 3 million individuals. *Nature Genetics, 54*, 437–449. https://doi.org/10.1038/s41588-022-01016-z

Trubetskoy, V., Pardiñas, A. F., Qi, T., Panagiotaropoulou, G., Awasthi, S., Bigdeli, T. B., Bryois, J., Chen, C.-Y., Dennison, C. A., Hall, L. S., Lam, M., Watanabe, K., Frei, O., Ge, T., Harwood, J. C., Koopmans, F., Magnusson, S., Richards, A. L., Sidorenko, J. … Schizophrenia Working Group of the Psychiatric Genomics Consortium. (2022). Mapping genomic loci implicates genes and synaptic biology in schizophrenia. *Nature, 604*, 502–508. https://doi.org/10.1038/s41586-022-04434-5

Chapter 10

From eye movements to sweaty hands

Psychobiological methods outside the brain

Introduction

In addition to neuroimaging and electrophysiological methods that measure brain activity, techniques assessing physiological processes or molecular markers outside of the brain represent a major group of key methodologies in psychobiology. This chapter will provide an overview of the main approaches in this area.

Measuring electrodermal activity to infer psychological states

Sweating is one of the body's major mechanisms for cooling down when the outside temperatures rise. However, a hot summer's day is not the only trigger: several psychological states can also induce sweating. Fear and nervousness are two examples of these. For example, people who are in anxiety-inducing situations, such as an important job interview, often experience sweaty hands. Being nervous before a first date with a crush can also result in intense sweating. Psychobiologists took note of these phenomena and developed a method to measure sweating to infer information about underlying processes. They measure **electrodermal activity (EDA)**, historically known as galvanic skin response, using two electrodes placed on different parts of the skin surface, which sends a very small electrical current between them. The resistance to that current is then measured in different experimental conditions (e.g., an emotional and a non-emotional condition). When someone sweats more, the resistance to the current lowers, as sweat mainly consists of water, which is a good conductor. The

Electrodermal activity (EDA): A measurement of the conductive properties of the skin using electrodes to infer an objective estimate of autonomic nervous system arousal.

DOI: 10.4324/9781003571537-13

rationale behind EDA is that sweating is not consciously controlled (we cannot increase our sweating by simply thinking that we want to sweat more) but controlled by the sympathetic nervous system, a part of the autonomic nervous system (see Chapter 2). When a person experiences psychological arousal from stress or emotions, activation of the autonomic nervous system increases sweating, which in turn decreases skin resistance. Note that the specific emotional state cannot be deduced from the method. For example, it is not clear whether someone is nervous due to fear or because of being in love. EDA allows for an objective measurement of emotional arousal that is less prone to subjective biases compared to self-reported questionnaires that a person can answer untruthfully for a variety of reasons. Because of this advantage, it comes as no surprise that EDA is used in a variety of psychobiological studies, focusing on topics such as fear conditioning, psychological correlates of pain, and emotional arousal.

EDA has also been used in research on the feeling of body ownership, for example, whether a person feels that a body part belongs to them. A common paradigm in this line of research is the so-called rubber hand illusion (Reinersmann et al., 2013). A person is placed sitting at a table, and a rubber arm (e.g., a medical arm prosthesis) is placed at a location at which one of the real arms would be. The real arm is then placed farther from the body than the rubber arm and hidden from the person's view using an occluder, like a piece of wooden board. Next, the experimenter strokes both the visible rubber hand and the hidden real hand synchronously with a paintbrush. At this point, many participants experience the rubber hand illusion, in which synchronous stroking creates the sensation that their real hand is located where the rubber hand is. To objectively measure how vivid the illusion is perceived, their EDA is measured while they observe the rubber hand being harmed, for example, by being stabbed with a syringe or hit with a hammer. The idea is that those who perceive the rubber hand illusion more strongly will have a more intense emotional reaction resulting in excessive EDA, compared to a control condition in which the illusion is not elicited.

Interestingly, measurement of the skin conductance response is also part of the polygraph, a pseudoscientific device that combines different measurements of physical parameters to work as a presumed lie-detector. The idea behind this device is that people sweat more when they lie compared to when they tell the truth. Although polygraph devices are sometimes featured in films and TV shows and used by some law enforcement agencies in the USA, the assumption that everyone sweats more when they lie is faulty, and many people can lie without an increase in sweating. Consequently, most countries do not allow the use of polygraph results as evidence in criminal cases today.

The electromyogram in psychology

Picture this: you are coming home to your apartment after a wonderful three-week holiday. You are well-rested, in high spirits, but feeling a bit hungry. You open your fridge and are immediately hit with the most revolting stench that fills your nostrils, making you wrinkle your nose in disgust. Before you lies a salmon steak you had forgotten to throw out the night before you left on holiday three weeks ago.

> **Electromyogram (EMG):** A measurement of the electric potentials that are generated by muscle cells.

Muscles make up a major part of the human body, with more than 600 individual ones identified. Importantly, emotional states are often accompanied by specific muscular changes, making the assessment of muscle activity an interesting tool for psychobiologists. Scientists can use an instrument called an electromyograph to record the **electromyogram (EMG)**, the electric potentials generated by muscle cells. While the EMG can be recorded for any muscle in the human body, psychobiologists often apply it to facial muscles. This is because many emotions are accompanied by specific activities of different muscle groups in the face. For example, smelling something rotten is often accompanied by a stereotypical "disgusted face", while people smile when they meet friends, or frown when something bad happens. These facial movement patterns are very similar across cultures, although their intensity can be affected by cultural norms. EMG has been widely used in psychobiological studies on facial emotions and is especially useful for objectively measuring emotions in infants, who cannot verbally report how they feel.

Measuring eye movements to assess the focus of attention

The eyes are one of the main sensory organs of the human body. In addition to allowing us to see the world around us, they also convey information about psychological states. You may have heard the expression "the eyes are the window to the soul". For example, assessing where someone is looking reveals their focus of attention. The eyes also express emotion in a variety of situations. For example, being happy and being sad are accompanied by specific eye movements. Whether someone looks another person in the eyes or averts their gaze can also reveal information about the relationship between these two individuals. Psychobiologists use a device called the **eye tracker** to measure eye movements (Carter & Luke,

2020). An eye tracker measures eye position and eye movements by recording the eyes with one or two cameras while infrared light is projected on the face and reflected by the cornea (the front of the eyeball). There are different types of eye trackers: many are head-mounted units, while others look like a box that is placed over a computer monitor. Some virtual reality headsets also have eye trackers included. The most important use of eye trackers in psychobiological research is that they allow to objectively determine focus of attention by measuring eye gaze, which makes it an essential tool in attention research. This is especially true when it comes to measuring the attention of infants. Eye tracking is also widely used in consumer psychology, for example, to determine which part of a web ad people spent the most attention on, or what product design details capture most attention. Moreover, eye tracking research is increasingly used in studies of people with autism. It has been shown that the proportion of fixation duration on eyes versus non-social areas when observing others can be used to discriminate between people with and without autism spectrum disorders (Setien-Ramos et al., 2023).

Eye tracker: A device that uses infrared light to create a reflection on the cornea that is filmed using cameras to determine eye fixation and eye movements.

Heart rate variability (HRV): The variation between heartbeats under the same physiological conditions. The HRV gets higher when people are relaxed and not stressed.

Heart rate and heart rate variability

We sometimes feel our hearts pounding in our chests during stressful situations. The heart rate reflects activation of the autonomic nervous system and has been shown to increase in response to emotional arousal. This can encompass both negative emotions (having a heated disagreement with a coworker) or positive emotions (being excited about going for coffee with a friend). While heart rate can be measured with an electrocardiogram (ECG), often used in a doctor's practice, it is typically measured using commercially available heart rate belts or sports watches in psychobiological experiments. Heart rate is often measured in experiments focused on stress or emotions. Many psychobiological studies also use a measure derived from the heart rate: the **heart variability (HRV)**. It works on the principle that variation between heartbeats is higher when people are relaxed and comfortable (Gullett et al., 2023). Reduced HRV has been linked to being stressed and worried and is also observed in some groups of patients, such as those with posttraumatic stress disorder.

Measuring hormones in psychological research

Hormones are amongst the most widely investigated classes of molecules in psychobiological research (see Chapter 3). Like neurotransmitters, hormones are signalling molecules. However, while neurotransmitters transmit information between a neuron and another cell at the synaptic cleft, hormones are produced in glands and secreted into the bloodstream and can be measured using saliva or blood samples. The research field within psychobiology that is focused on how hormones interact with the brain and psychological conditions is called **psychoneuroendocrinology.** The largest area of psychobiological research involving hormonal measurements is stress research (Pfeifer et al., 2021), with cortisol being the major stress hormone (see Chapter 18). However, stress hormones are not the only hormones measured in psychobiological research. Other major classes of commonly investigated hormones include bonding hormones such as oxytocin and vasopressin (see Chapter 14), female sex hormones such as oestradiol and progesterone, as well as male sex hormones like testosterone (Hausmann, 2017). Female sex hormones are often measured in studies examining how the menstrual cycle affects psychological processes, including attention, emotion, sleep, pain processing, and more.

> **Psychoneuroendocrinology**: A research area within psychobiology that is focused on the interaction between hormones, brain structure and function, and psychological processes.

Immune system parameters and psychological processes

Did you ever experience getting physically sick after an intensely stressful episode, such as taking several exams within a short time span? This is quite a common experience and shows that the immune system, while mainly being relevant in the context of physical illnesses, is affected by psychological factors. The research area within psychobiology that is focused on the interaction between the immune system, brain structure and function, and psychological processes is called **psychoneuroimmunology**. Psychologists can determine the level of various molecules relevant to the immune system from blood samples or other samples that are collected from volunteers who participate in experiments. These include, for example, various forms of interleukins, small proteins that regulate inflammation processes in response to infections, interferon gamma, a protein that regulates the immune response, and tumour necrosis factor alpha, a messenger molecule that triggers inflammation. The main focus of psychoneuroimmunology is to understand how psychological stress (see Chapter 18) can affect bodily function to have an impact on physical health. In general, the major stress systems of the body and the immune system affect each other in complex ways. On the one hand, immune system molecules that regulate inflammation increase cortisol release, but cortisol also reduces the production of certain pro-inflammatory molecules. Therefore, measuring immune system parameters is a meaningful addition to any psychobiological study on stress.

Psychoneuroimmunology: A research area within psychobiology that is focused on the interaction between the immune system, brain structure and function, and psychological processes.

Conclusion

While the brain is often the focus of psychobiological research, several methods have been developed to measure other biological processes in the body that are relevant for psychological functioning. The most widely used ones include the measurement of eye movements, muscle activity, EDA, immune parameters, and hormone measurements. Many of these methods reveal information about the activity of the autonomic nervous system and have the advantage that they objectively measure psychological parameters such as attention, allocation, or emotional arousal in a way that cannot be consciously controlled by the participants. This makes them less prone to participant biases.

Further reading

Additional academic source: Daruna, J. H. (2012). *Introduction to Psychoneuroimmunology*. Academic Press.

Relevant web resource: https://www.sciencedirect.com/journal/psychoneuroendocrinology/, the website of the academic journal *Psychoneuroendocrinology*.

References

Carter, B. T., & Luke, S. G. (2020). Best practices in eye tracking research. *International Journal of Psychophysiology: Official Journal of the International Organization of Psychophysiology, 155*, 49–62. https://doi.org/10.1016/j.ijpsycho.2020.05.010

Gullett, N., Zajkowska, Z., Walsh, A., Harper, R., & Mondelli, V. (2023). Heart rate variability (HRV) as a way to understand associations between the autonomic nervous system (ANS) and affective states: a critical review of the literature. *International Journal of Psychophysiology: Official Journal of the International Organization of Psychophysiology, 192*, 35–42. https://doi.org/10.1016/j.ijpsycho.2023.08.001

Hausmann, M. (2017). Why sex hormones matter for neuroscience: a very short review on sex, sex hormones, and functional brain asymmetries. *Journal of Neuroscience Research, 95*, 40–49. https://doi.org/10.1002/jnr.23857

Pfeifer, L. S., Heyers, K., Ocklenburg, S., & Wolf, O. T. (2021). Stress research during the COVID-19 pandemic and beyond. *Neuroscience and Biobehavioral Reviews, 131*, 581–596. https://doi.org/10.1016/j.neubiorev.2021.09.045

Reinersmann, A., Landwehrt, J., Krumova, E. K., Peterburs, J., Ocklenburg, S., Güntürkün, O., & Maier, C. (2013). The rubber hand illusion in complex regional pain syndrome: preserved ability to integrate a rubber hand indicates intact multisensory integration. *Pain, 154,* 1519–1527. https://doi.org/10.1016/j.pain.2013.03.039

Setien-Ramos, I., Lugo-Marín, J., Gisbert-Gustemps, L., Díez-Villoria, E., Magán-Maganto, M., Canal-Bedia, R., & Ramos-Quiroga, J. A. (2023). Eye-tracking studies in adults with autism spectrum disorder: a systematic review and meta-analysis. *Journal of Autism and Developmental Disorders, 53*, 2430–2443. https://doi.org/10.1007/s10803-022-05524-z

Chapter 11

Stimulate my brain

Transcranial magnetic stimulation and other neuromodulation techniques

Introduction

Some methodologies in psychobiology allow us to modulate or alter brain activity. These methods are highly informative because they can temporarily increase or decrease neural activity. Unlike other brain mapping techniques, such as an electroencephalogram (see Chapter 7) or functional magnetic resonance imaging (see Chapter 8), which only show correlations with behaviour, these **neuromodulation** methods enables scientists to observe **cause-and-effect relationships**. In this chapter, we highlight three non-invasive and two invasive key methodologies in psychobiology that modulate neural activation in the brain.

Cause-and-effect relationships: A relationship in which one event or variable (the cause) directly leads to a change in another (the effect).

Transcranial magnetic stimulation (TMS): A non-invasive method that uses magnetic fields to stimulate nerve cells in specific brain regions.

Non-invasive brain stimulation

Non-invasive brain stimulation is a set of techniques used to modulate brain activity without the need for surgical interventions and does not result in lasting harm to the tissue being stimulated. It includes methods such as transcranial magnetic stimulation (TMS), transcranial direct current stimulation (tDCS), and transcranial alternating current stimulation (tACS). These approaches are increasingly used in psychobiological research and in clinical practice to explore brain mechanisms, enhance cognitive functions, and treat neurological disorders.

DOI: 10.4324/9781003571537-14

Transcranial magnetic stimulation

The most widely used neuromodulation method in psychobiology is **TMS**, which was introduced in the 1980s. Figure 11.1 shows a typical TMS setup with the stimulation coil positioned over the participant's head.

In TMS, a coil is placed on or near the scalp. The TMS coil generates a rapidly changing magnetic field that induces an electric current in the underlying cortical tissue. This current can depolarise neurons (making their membrane potential less negative), thereby modulating brain activity. The shape and orientation of the coil determine how focal the induced current is. In the most common figure-of-eight coil, the magnetic field is strongest near the midpoint of the two loops, enabling relatively focused stimulation over an area of about 1 cm^3. For instance, a single pulse applied over the primary motor cortex can cause a visible twitch in a finger by activating neurons whose axons project to the

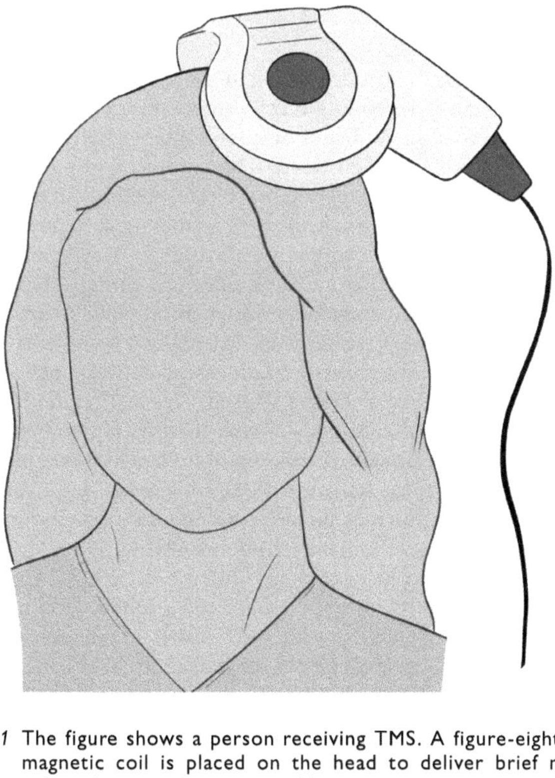

Figure 11.1 The figure shows a person receiving TMS. A figure-eight-shaped magnetic coil is placed on the head to deliver brief magnetic pulses that stimulate targeted brain regions.

spinal cord and then to the muscles of the hand. This is an example of single-pulse TMS. **Single-pulse TMS** emits a single brief magnetic pulse that triggers a short burst of neural activity (around 10 ms), followed by a transient period of reduced excitability (around 100–200 ms). It therefore only causes a very brief disruption of ongoing neural processing. Instead, **repetitive TMS (rTMS)** delivers a series of pulses over a longer period of time. This can produce more long-lasting effects, from 30 minutes to several days, depending on the stimulation duration. rTMS can also be utilised to either enhance or inhibit brain activity, depending on the pattern of pulses administered. The choice of stimulation pattern depends on the intended experimental or therapeutic outcome.

> **Single-pulse TMS:** A technique that delivers a single brief magnetic pulse to the brain, producing a brief burst of cortical activity (about 10 ms) followed by a short period of reduced cortical excitability (about 100–200 ms).
>
> **Repetitive TMS (rTMS):** A technique that delivers a series of magnetic pulses to the brain, producing longer-lasting changes in cortical excitability that can persist from about 30 minutes to several days, depending on the stimulation protocol.

When the induced electric field alters membrane potentials and influences neuronal firing, the temporary disruption is sometimes called a "virtual lesion". However, stimulation does not entirely stop neural firing; instead, it leads to irregular or desynchronised activity, disrupting normal coordinated firing patterns in that region. Because of this, TMS is a useful tool for testing causal relationships between brain areas and cognitive functions. If stimulating a specific cortical region impairs performance on a particular task, it suggests that the region is essential for that function. For example, researchers found rTMS over the anterior temporal lobes disrupted semantic tasks (knowledge about the meaning of words or objects) such as picture naming and word comprehension, but not tasks without a semantic component, indicating that this area is key for semantic representation (Pobric et al., 2007). Unlike lesion studies, TMS allows for within-subject comparisons in healthy individuals by evaluating performance with and without stimulation. It is widely used in biopsychological studies of language, attention, memory, decision making, and motor control. TMS can also be used to explore brain plasticity and reorganisation after, for example, a stroke, or in cases of sensory deprivation, such as the organisation of the visual cortex in blind individuals. Recently, there has also been significant interest in applying TMS therapeutically. For example, TMS is now frequently offered as a treatment option for treatment-resistant depression that persists despite medication. Here, stimulation of the left dorsolateral prefrontal cortex is believed to create neuroplastic changes in prefrontal and limbic circuits which influence mood regulation.

TMS is most effective on cortical structures because it is not possible to stimulate deeper brain regions without affecting surface neurons. Since TMS alters brain function, it must be used carefully. For example, early research during its development showed that improper use could trigger seizures in individuals with no prior history. It may also cause headaches, muscle twitches, and nausea. Therefore, following strict guidelines is essential to ensure the procedure remains safe with only mild potential side effects.

Transcranial direct current stimulation

Transcranial direct current stimulation (tDCS) involves applying a weak electrical current to influence neuronal excitability (Narmashiri & Akbari, 2025). It can either enhance (facilitatory) or suppress (inhibitory) neural activity. Typically, two electrodes are placed on the participant's scalp, with one designated as the target electrode and the other as the reference. During stimulation, current flows between the electrodes and passes through the brain to complete the circuit. Anodal (positive) stimulation depolarises neurons, increasing the likelihood of action potentials and thereby facilitating behaviour. Conversely, cathodal (negative) stimulation hyperpolarises neurons, reducing the probability of action potentials and inhibiting behaviour. The direction of current flow between the electrodes determines which condition is being used. In psychobiological experiments, the "active" condition is typically compared to a "sham" condition, where no stimulation occurs. For example, in one study, researchers used anodal (facilitatory) tDCS over the right orbitofrontal cortex in adults. Participants then performed a facial expression task with either emotional or neutral expressions during stimulation or sham (Willis et al., 2015). Results showed that participants were both more accurate and quicker at labelling expressions during stimulation,

> **Transcranial direct current stimulation (tDCS)**: A non-invasive method that applies gentle electrical currents to the scalp to modulate neuronal excitability.
>
> **Transcranial alternating current stimulation (tACS)**: A non-invasive method that applies alternating electrical currents to modulate neural oscillations.

indicating that this technique could help treat facial expression recognition issues caused by damage or dysfunction in the orbitofrontal cortex.

tDCS is a practical method because it is relatively inexpensive. However, the results may vary, partly because of differences in methodological approaches across studies. Going forward, pinpointing the optimal conditions for tDCS application will be essential for creating precise and effective cognitive enhancement strategies with this non-invasive brain stimulation method.

Transcranial alternating current stimulation

The brain naturally produces rhythmic waves called neural oscillations, which result from the ongoing balance between brain cells that excite or inhibit each other. **tACS** is a non-invasive technique used to try to influence these brain rhythms (Wischnewski et al, 2023). This is carried out by placing two or more electrodes on the scalp and skin to deliver mild oscillating electrical currents, typically between 1 and 4 mA. The currents that reach the brain are very weak because the skull conducts electricity poorly, and a portion of the applied current is diverted through surrounding tissues, such as the skin and cerebrospinal fluid, before reaching the brain. Therefore, they do not directly induce or increase the likelihood of action potentials, such as TMS or tDCS. Instead, they attempt to influence the timing of neuronal firing by rhythmically shifting membrane potentials. This is called **entrainment**: a process in which one system's signal or oscillation naturally synchronises with another. In the case of tACS, this means the brain's ongoing activity aligns with the external alternating current. In this way, scientists can influence various things: the strength of the rhythms, how quickly they occur, and how well different brain areas stay in sync. There is also some evidence that such modulation can lead to lasting, plasticity-related effects even after the stimulation has ended.

> **Entrainment**: A process in which one system's signal or oscillation naturally synchronises with another.
>
> **Deep brain stimulation (DBS)**: An invasive procedure involving the surgical implantation of electrodes into the brain to deliver electrical pulses to targeted areas.

tACS is a safe procedure with minimal side effects, such as tingling sensations. It is also affordable and portable, making it suitable for home use. It can be customised with specific settings and electrode placements based on individual brains. However, since the currents are very weak, they only influence the outer brain layers. As tACS is relatively new in psychobiological research, scientists are still exploring the best ways to use the method effectively.

Invasive brain stimulation

Invasive electrical stimulation techniques require surgically implanting the stimulation device into the patient, either directly into the brain or into the nerves that connect to the brain. Two examples of invasive brain stimulation are deep brain stimulation (DBS) and vagus nerve stimulation (VNS).

Deep brain stimulation

DBS involves surgically placing small wires or electrodes into the brain to deliver targeted electrical pulses. These electrodes connect to a neurostimulator, powered by a battery, which is implanted under the collarbone, similar to a pacemaker. The device continuously transmits electrical impulses through the leads into the brain. Typically, DBS is considered only after other treatment options have failed, due to its risks, since the surgeon must navigate through brain tissue to reach the target site. Therefore, a careful evaluation of risks and benefits is essential before the procedure.

DBS has been used to treat conditions such as Parkinson's disease, a progressive neurodegenerative disorder. The primary symptom of Parkinson's is bradykinesia, which involves the slowing of voluntary actions (such as crossing legs) and automatic movements (like swinging while walking). About 20% of patients also experience tremors, and other symptoms include cognitive decline and depression (Bloem et al., 2021). In Parkinson's disease, the nerve cells in the substantia nigra that produce dopamine die faster than in a healthy brain, leading to these symptoms. The initial treatment for Parkinson's disease involves dopaminergic medications, like Levodopa, to boost dopamine levels. If these medications fail, DBS is considered. DBS works by delivering electrical impulses to brain tissue to modulate or disrupt neural activity in specific areas. The most common targets are in the subthalamic nucleus or globus pallidus, both part of the basal ganglia. While DBS does not completely cure Parkinson's disease or other conditions, it can reduce medication requirements and improve quality of life.

Vagus nerve stimulation

The vagus nerve, also known as Cranial Nerve X, is a **cranial nerve** that originates directly from the brain or brainstem and is the longest nerve in the body. The left and right vagus nerves originate in the brainstem and extend down through the neck and chest into the abdomen, sending branches to several organs, including the heart, lungs, and digestive system. Signals from the vagus nerve travel back to the brain and end in the nucleus tractus solitarius, which connects directly or indirectly to various brain regions, including the amygdala, hypothalamus, thalamus, and orbitofrontal cortex. The vagus nerve is made up of approximately 20% efferent fibres that send signals from the brain to the body, and 80% afferent fibres that carry information from the body to the brain. The main functions include regulating heart rate, promoting digestion, controlling mood and stress responses, and supporting immune function.

> **Cranial nerve**: A nerve that originates directly from the brain or brainstem.

Vagus nerve stimulation (VNS) involves surgically placing bipolar electrodes on the left cervical branch of the vagus nerve. The left vagus nerve is used more often than the right because the right vagus nerve is more likely to have branches to the heart. Electrical pulses are delivered via an implanted pulse generator in the chest. While this procedure is invasive, it is typically safe with minimal risks and few side effects. VNS was initially developed to treat non-treatment-responsive epilepsy. However, it was noted early that it brought beneficial side effects. For example, a study involving children with epilepsy found that although VNS did not reduce seizure duration or frequency, it did improve general behaviour and mood. These beneficial side effects prompted further research into VNS for depression, which has shown some promising results in individuals with treatment-resistant depression (Austelle et al., 2022).

> **Vagus nerve stimulation (VNS)**: An invasive method in which electrical pulses are delivered to the vagus nerve through implanted electrodes to influence brain function.

One of the main barriers to VNS is its high cost and invasive nature. Recently, a non-invasive alternative called **transcutaneous auricular vagus nerve stimulation (taVNS)** has been developed. In taVNS, electrodes are placed on specific areas of the ear believed to be connected to the **auricular branch of the vagus nerve**. Although researchers

> **Transcutaneous auricular vagus nerve stimulation (taVNS):** A non-invasive method in which the vagus nerve is stimulated via electrodes placed on the ear.

> **Auricular branch of the vagus nerve:** A small branch of the vagus nerve that carries sensory info from part of the outer ear to the brain. Its superficial location means low-amplitude electrical stimulation at the skin surface can create electric fields deep enough to modify its activity.

are still identifying the best stimulation sites, the most common are the tragus (the front part of the outer ear canal) and the cymba conchae (Badran et al., 2019). While the technique is still evolving and optimal stimulation parameters are under investigation, it shows promise for future applications in areas where VNS has been successful, such as the treatment of tinnitus, epilepsy, and depression.

Conclusion

Neuromodulation techniques open exciting new avenues for advancing psychobiological research and developing innovative treatments. As this field continues to evolve, it is crucial to consider safety and ethical standards for future initiatives. Organisations like the Neurorights Foundation will no doubt play a vital role in guiding the responsible development and application of neurotechnologies and neuromodulation methods in the future.

> **Neuromodulation techniques:** Techniques that directly alter brain activity.

Further reading

Additional academic source: Chaudhary, U. (2025). Invasive brain stimulation techniques. In: *Expanding Senses using Neurotechnology*. Springer Nature. https://doi.org/10.1007/978-3-031-76081-5_7

Additional academic source: Chen, R., Fitzgerald, P. B., & Blumberger, D. M. (2022). *A Practical Guide to Transcranial Magnetic Stimulation Neurophysiology and Treatment Studies*. Oxford University Press.

Additional academic source: Loo, C. K. (2021). *Transcranial Direct Current Stimulation in Neuropsychiatric Disorders: Clinical Principles and Management*. Springer.

Relevant web resource: https://neurorightsfoundation.org/, the website of the nonprofit *Neurorights Foundation*, created to ensure the ethical development and deployment of neurotechnologies.

References

Austelle, C. W., O'Leary, G. H., Thompson, S., Gruber, E., Kahn, A., Manett, A. J., Short, B., & Badran, B. W. (2022). A comprehensive review of vagus nerve stimulation for depression. *Neuromodulation: Technology at the Neural Interface, 25*(3), 309–315. https://doi.org/10.1111/ner.13528

Badran, B. W., Alfred, B. Y., Adair, D., Mappin, G., DeVries, W. H., Jenkins, D. D., George, M. S., & Bikson, M. (2019). Laboratory administration of transcutaneous auricular vagus nerve stimulation (taVNS): technique, targeting, and considerations. *Journal of Visualized Experiments: JoVE*, (143), 10.3791. https://doi.org/10.3791/58984

Bloem, B. R., Okun, M. S., & Klein, C. (2021). Parkinson's disease. *The Lancet, 397*(10291), 2284–2303.

Narmashiri, A., & Akbari, F. (2025). The effects of transcranial direct current stimulation (tDCS) on the cognitive functions: a systematic review and meta-analysis. *Neuropsychology Review, 35*(1), 126–152. https://doi.org/10.1007/s11065-023-09627-x

Pobric, G., Jefferies, E., & Ralph, M. A. L. (2007). Anterior temporal lobes mediate semantic representation: mimicking semantic dementia by using rTMS in normal participants. *Proceedings of the National Academy of Sciences, 104*(50), 20137–20141. https://doi.org/10.1073/pnas.0707383104

Willis, M. L., Murphy, J. M., Ridley, N. J., & Vercammen, A. (2015). Anodal tDCS targeting the right orbitofrontal cortex enhances facial expression recognition. *Social Cognitive and Affective Neuroscience, 10*(12), 1677–1683. https://doi.org/10.1093/scan/nsv057

Wischnewski, M., Alekseichuk, I., & Opitz, A. (2023). Neurocognitive, physiological, and biophysical effects of. *Trends in Cognitive Sciences, 27*(2), 189–205. https://doi.org/10.1016/j.tics.2022.11.013

Section 4

Key impacts on research or practice and policy

This section gives an overview of the key impacts that psychobiological research has in tackling major societal problems such as dementia, stress, and addiction. It will also highlight research areas in which psychobiological research has led to major insights, including social neuroscience, the psychobiology of hunger, understanding animal behaviour, and neurodiversity.

At the end of section four, you will:

- Have gained basic insights into the psychobiology of memory and dementia
- Have learned about the psychobiology underlying addiction
- Have gained knowledge of the biological principles underlying bonding and social interaction
- Understand hunger from a psychobiological perspective
- Have an overview of current insights on how animal brains work
- Be able to discuss the current state of knowledge about brain individuality and neurodiversity
- Understand how the brain responds to stress in acute and chronic situations

DOI: 10.4324/9781003571537-15

Chapter 12

Lost minds

Psychobiological research on memory in the time of ageing societies and Alzheimer's disease

Introduction

> **Neurodegenerative disease**: A neurological disease that is characterised by a progressively worsening loss of neurons in the brain and sometimes also the peripheral nervous system.

If you reflect on your life, what is your favourite memory? For many people, answers to this question include the birth of a sibling or child, the day a new pet joined the family, a first kiss, holidays, weddings, or career milestones such as obtaining a university degree. Our memories are the very core of our existence. Who would we be without the ability to recall our names, conversations with loved ones, and travels with friends? However, losing these memories is a tragic reality for many people with **neurodegenerative diseases** such as Alzheimer's disease (AD), Parkinson's disease, and Huntington's disease. In general, neurodegenerative diseases are characterised by the progressive loss of neurons in the brain, and in some cases, the peripheral nervous system. These conditions are largely incurable, but some symptoms can be relieved temporarily by medication. As many neurodegenerative diseases get progressively worse with age, they represent a growing societal problem as the average human lifespan is increasing. In this chapter, we focus on the most common neurodegenerative disease that is also the one that most profoundly disrupts our ability to retain memories: AD. We then explore psychobiological research on the different memory systems in the brain and consider how these findings could help us understand the enormous societal challenge caused by neurodegenerative diseases.

Forgetting who we are: AD and dementia

Over the last century, life expectancy at birth in many high-income nations has risen by about 30 years (Olshansky et al., 2024). While an increased

DOI: 10.4324/9781003571537-16

Dementia: A syndrome caused by neurodegenerative diseases characterised by problems with memory, thinking, behaviour, emotions, and motivation.

Alzheimer's disease (AD): A neurodegenerative disease characterised by memory loss.

Mild cognitive impairment (MCI): A state in which a person shows problems with memory and cognition that are worse than expected at their age.

Neurodegeneration: Progressive and irreversible loss of neurons due to cell death.

average lifespan is, of course, a positive development, it also brings unique challenges for societies and health care systems. One of the major societal challenges worldwide in this regard is **dementia**. Dementia is not a disease itself, but a syndrome caused by AD and other neurodegenerative disorders. It is most prominently characterised by memory problems (particularly towards recent events), but also other difficulties affecting thinking, behaviour, emotion, and motivation. Patients with severe dementia are often unable to perform even basic everyday activities such as personal hygiene, shopping, or cooking, and often rely completely on the care of others. While the prevalence of dementia was approximately 50 million people worldwide over the past decade, it is projected to triple by 2050 (Scheltens et al., 2021). In the UK, about 982,000 people were estimated to live with dementia in 2024 (Alzheimer's Society, 2024). The most prominent cause for dementia is **AD** (Scheltens et al., 2021), named after the German Alois Alzheimer (1864–1915), who first described the condition. At the symptom level, AD is primarily characterised by memory loss, particularly for recent events, while many core memories from childhood and adolescence often remain intact. Further problems affecting thinking, orientation, behaviour, emotion, and motivation are commonly observed as AD progresses. The disease typically develops on a continuum: healthy people show small issues with memory and thinking. This then develops into a state called **mild cognitive impairment (MCI)**, in which the person shows problems with memory and cognition worse than expected at their age. MCI then slowly progresses into AD. On the brain level, AD is characterised by **neurodegeneration**, the progressive and irreversible loss of neurons due to cell death. This primarily affects the medial temporal lobe, including the hippocampus, which is a central structure in memory (see below), but also the frontal and parietal lobes, as well as other brain structures. Figure 12.1 shows a comparison between a healthy brain and that of a patient with AD.

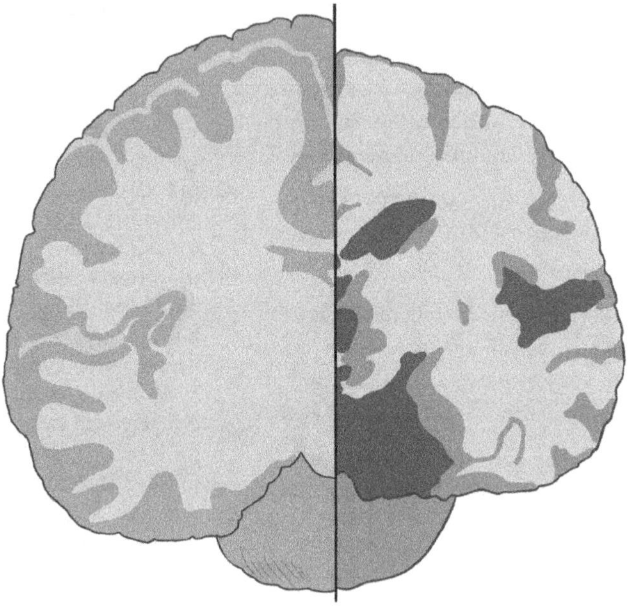

Figure 12.1 Compared to a healthy brain (left side), a brain affected by Alzheimer's disease shows massive neurodegeneration (shrinking due to death of neurons) and enlargement of ventricles (cavities in the brain filled with fluid).

Amyloid-beta plaques: A deposit of misfolded proteins in AD that is thought to cause neurodegeneration.

Neurofibrillary tangles: A clump of misfolded proteins in AD that is thought to cause neurodegeneration.

What causes the widespread death of nerve cells in AD? In the brains of individuals with AD, two types of misfolded proteins can be found that kill nerve cells. First, there are **amyloid-beta plaques**. Amyloid-beta is a protein that normally exists in the brain. However, in AD, the protein is abnormally folded into plaques: rigid deposits that accumulate in the grey matter of the brain. The amyloid-beta plaques are believed to be neurotoxic and to trigger neurodegeneration. In addition to amyloid-beta plaques, the brains of patients with AD also show **neurofibrillary tangles** (large clumps of proteins in neurons) that consist of misfolded tau protein. In its normal form, tau is relevant for the stability of axons. These neurofibrillary tangles are also neurotoxic and cause neurodegeneration. Although AD typically occurs after the age of 65 years, a rare form called early-onset AD can cause the disease to break out as early as the 40s. People with early-onset AD often have a family history of memory problems (e.g., their parents reported memory problems early on or have a confirmed diagnosis of AD). In general, AD is highly heritable, with the disease risk depending 58% to 79% on heritable factors (Gatz et al., 2006). There are more than 40 AD risk alleles, with the most prominent one being the E4 allele on the Apolipoprotein E (*APOE*) gene. Apolipoprotein E is a protein that plays a role in the breakdown of amyloid-beta. This process works less efficiently in people with the E4 allele, which may lead to more amyloid-beta plaques in their brains. Consequently, the *APOE* E4 allele is associated with a 3–4 times higher risk of developing AD compared to individuals without it. There is currently no cure for AD, as neurodegeneration cannot be reversed. Future treatment approaches will have to focus on the early detection of individual biological risk factors. One promising, but speculative, line of research is the development of mRNA-based vaccines for AD that aim to prevent pathological amyloid-beta plaque build-up before it occurs, thus preventing neurodegeneration (Hovakimyan et al., 2024). One thing is clear: only through substantial investment in basic and clinical science will we be able to solve the issue of AD and prevent immense individual suffering and societal burden.

The psychobiology of working memory

While experimental research on memory has classically been a domain of cognitive psychology, psychobiological research has contributed significantly to our understanding of the brain structures underlying memory. There is not only one memory network in the brain, but instead several interacting networks with partly overlapping brain areas that represent the different forms of memory. In general, memory networks that hold information for a longer time (sometimes for life) and memory networks that hold information for a shorter time (like seconds to minutes) can be distinguished.

Imagine meeting someone at a party and starting a vivid conversation about pizza. You really enjoy talking to them, and at some point, they take out their smartphone to show you a glorious picture of a pineapple pizza on their social media. You want to follow their account but feel it would be a bit too forward to do so immediately. Instead, you take note of their social media handle, memorise and rehearse it until you can sneak away and write it down so you can follow them the next day.

What happened in this example is that you used your **working memory** to keep the information about the social media handle in your mind until you were able to write it down. The working memory is a memory network that has limited storage capacity (you can remember one social media handle like that but not 50 at the same time) and is used to store information that is needed for the execution of a plan (writing the handle down) for a short time (you can remember the social media handle for minutes, but not for days). Psychobiological research has shown that the core brain structure in working memory is the prefrontal cortex in the frontal lobe (D'Esposito & Postle, 2015). The prefrontal cortex recruits networks that normally process the stimulus to be retained in working memory (such as visual networks for remembering a picture or auditory networks for remembering spoken words).

Working memory: Working memory is a memory network that has limited storage capacity and is used to store information that is needed for the execution of a plan for a short time.

Explicit memory: Conscious and verbalisable long-term memory, including episodic and semantic memory.

Implicit memory: Unconscious and procedural memory, such as the ability to swim.

Episodic memory: A long-term memory network focused on remembering past experiences from one's own life.

Semantic memory: A long-term memory network focused on remembering general facts about the world independent of personal experience.

The psychobiology of explicit and implicit memory

In addition to working memory, the brain has several memory networks dedicated to long-term storage of information. These can be divided into **explicit memory** (conscious and verbalisable memory) and **implicit memory** (unconscious and procedural memory that cannot be easily put into words). Explicit memory includes **episodic memory** (remembering past experiences from one's own life, like the first day of high school) and **semantic memory** (remembering general facts about the world independent of personal experience, such as the lyrics to a specific song).

The key brain structure for episodic memory is the **hippocampus** in the medial temporal lobe (Kolibius et al., 2025). The hippocampus

Hippocampus: A brain structure in the medial temporal lobe that is crucial for episodic memory.

does, however, not store the memories itself. Instead, groups of connected neurons in the hippocampus link representations of different parts of a memory in the cortex. How important the hippocampus is for episodic memory has been shown by the famous case of Henry Molaison (1926–2008), also known as "H.M.". Doctors treating H.M. decided to remove large parts of both the left and the right temporal lobes, including large parts of both hippocampi, to control treatment-resistant epilepsy. This resulted in the inability for H.M. to form new episodic memories after the time point of the surgery.

Implicit memory refers to several different perceptual and motor skills that are typically much harder to verbalise than episodic or semantic memories. Implicit memory includes procedural motor skills like knowing how to swim without drowning or how to use a smartphone. These skills do not rely heavily on the hippocampus but are largely mediated by the networks between the basal ganglia, particularly the striatum, and the cortex (Kreitzer et al., 2008). The dissociation of explicit and implicit memory was also evident in H.M., who, despite severe episodic memory problems, had largely intact implicit memory.

Intentional and unintentional forgetting

Memories can be beautiful and moving and an enormous source of happiness in life, but they can also be traumatic and stressful. For this reason, people sometimes wish they could intentionally forget certain memories. In contrast, for people with dementia, we typically want to prevent the person from forgetting. Whether we retain a memory for a long time or not depends to some extent on Hebbian learning (see Chapter 4). For example, we are more likely to remember a person we have seen every day for years compared to someone we only saw once. This is because the cell ensembles associated with the memory of the person we see often fire often and repeatedly, strengthening their associations. However, the emotional arousal in the situation also plays an important role: a one-time traumatic event that elicited strong negative emotions can be remembered very vividly for decades.

Conclusion

AD represents a growing societal challenge worldwide. Psychobiological research can help us understand these diseases better, for example, by identifying the neural bases of memories in healthy brains.

Further reading

Additional academic source: Baddeley, A., Eysenck, M., & Anderson, M. C. (2025). *Memory* (4th ed.). Routledge.

Additional academic source: Innes, A., O'Connell, M. E., Geoghegan, C., & Fehr, P. (2025). *How to Live Well with Dementia Expert Help for People Living with Dementia and their Family, Friends, and Care Partners.* Routledge.

Relevant web resource: https://www.alzheimers.org.uk/, the website of the *Alzheimer's Society.*

Relevant web resource: https://www.cam.ac.uk/stories/cambridge-onfire-dementia-blood-test, a report from the University of Cambridge about how blood tests could help in detecting dementia before it starts to slow down disease progression.

Related film: *Still Alice* (2014). A moving film about a linguistics professor suffering from Alzheimer's disease.

Related film: *Eternal sunshine of the spotless mind* (2004). A science fiction drama about memory erasure.

References

Alzheimer's Society. (2024). *How many people have dementia in the UK?* Alzheimer's Society. https://www.alzheimers.org.uk/cy/node/42286

D'Esposito, M., & Postle, B. R. (2015). The cognitive neuroscience of working memory. *Annual Review of Psychology, 66*, 115–142. https://doi.org/10.1146/annurev-psych-010814-015031

Gatz, M., Reynolds, C. A., Fratiglioni, L., Johansson, B., Mortimer, J. A., Berg, S., Fiske, A., & Pedersen, N. L. (2006). Role of genes and environments for explaining Alzheimer disease. *Archives of General Psychiatry, 63*, 168–174. https://doi.org/10.1001/archpsyc.63.2.168

Hovakimyan, A., Chilingaryan, G., King, O., Capocchi, J. K., Chadarevian, J. P., Davtyan, H., Kniazev, R., Agadjanyan, M. G., & Ghochikyan, A. (2024). mRNA Vaccine for Alzheimer's disease: pilot study. *Vaccines, 12*, 659. https://doi.org/10.3390/vaccines12060659

Kolibius, L. D., Josselyn, S. A., & Hanslmayr, S. (2025). On the origin of memory neurons in the human hippocampus. *Trends in Cognitive Sciences, 29*, 421–433. https://doi.org/10.1016/j.tics.2025.01.013

Kreitzer, A. C., & Malenka, R. C. (2008). Striatal plasticity and basal ganglia circuit function. *Neuron, 60*, 543–554. https://doi.org/10.1016/j.neuron.2008.11.005

Olshansky, S. J., Willcox, B. J., Demetrius, L., & Beltrán-Sánchez, H. (2024). Implausibility of radical life extension in humans in the twenty-first century. *Nature Aging, 4*, 1635–1642. https://doi.org/10.1038/s43587-024-00702-3

Scheltens, P., De Strooper, B., Kivipelto, M., Holstege, H., Chételat, G., Teunissen, C. E., Cummings, J., & van der Flier, W. M. (2021). Alzheimer's disease. *Lancet, 397*, 1577–1590. https://doi.org/10.1016/S0140-6736(20)32205-4

Chapter 13

I want to stop, but I cannot

The psychobiology of addiction in times of the opioid crisis (and social media)

Introduction

In 1959, a substance called fentanyl was first synthesised in Belgium. This strong opioid painkiller is up to 50 times more potent than heroin, and doctors primarily use it to manage pain in post-surgery wound treatment, palliative care, and cancer treatment. Because of its effectiveness in treating otherwise unbearable pain, the World Health Organization lists fentanyl on its Model List of Essential Medicines. However, fentanyl also has another, far darker, side. The U.S. National Center for Health Statistics (2025) reported over 80,000 drug overdose deaths in the U.S. alone in 2024. Of those, synthetic opioids, with the main drug in this category being fentanyl, caused over 48,000 overdoses, making them the leading cause of overdose fatality. Methamphetamine and other psychostimulants caused over 29,000 overdoses, followed by cocaine (including crack), which accounted for over 22,000 overdoses. The reason why fentanyl is especially dangerous is due to its extremely high effectiveness: it poses a high risk of deadly side effects even at very low doses, including severely reducing breathing, which can quickly lead to death if not treated. Although the deadly effects of fentanyl have been known for decades, hundreds of thousands of people in the U.S. alone still abuse it as a recreational drug because it produces an intense, short-term rush of euphoria. Understanding why so many people risk their jobs, relationships, and ultimately, their lives, for a quick, short-lived rush is a psychobiological research question of utmost societal importance. In addition, opioids are not the only thing people are addicted to. Addiction can occur to a variety of substances, with the most common ones being caffeine, tobacco, and alcohol. Others include cannabinoids, stimulants such as cocaine, sedatives, hallucinogens, inhalants, and many more. There are also many non-substance-related activities that can be addictive, from gambling to sex, video games, exercise, and social media use. In this chapter, we will highlight how psychobiological research can help us understand the hows and whys of addiction and why some people cannot stop even if they so desperately want to.

DOI: 10.4324/9781003571537-17

The psychobiology of acute drug use: the example of fentanyl

To understand why some people enjoy taking drugs and may eventually develop an addiction, it is crucial to consider how the reward system of the brain works. Let us use fentanyl as an example. As fentanyl is an opiate, it binds to opiate receptors in the central nervous system. There are four different main types of opioid receptors called mu, kappa, delate, and zeta. All four of them are found in several different brain areas. One of their main functions is pain modulation, hence the use of many opioids as painkillers. The **mu opioid receptor** plays a crucial role in producing the euphoric effects when using fentanyl (Chaudun et al., 2024). This receptor can be found in neurons that express γ-aminobutyric acid or GABA (a major inhibitory neurotransmitter in the brain) in the **ventral tegmental area (VTA)**. The VTA is a group of neurons in the midbrain. The VTA contains a large number of dopaminergic cells, the neurons that produce and release **dopamine**, and is the main structure from which dopaminergic axons project into the rest of the brain. Since the reward system crucially relies on the excitatory neurotransmitter dopamine, the VTA is a core area in the brain's reward network. Dopamine signals the brain whether something is desirable or not and contributes to the subjective feelings of pleasure and euphoria. Rewarding stimuli, as well as many abused drugs, increase dopamine levels. There are three major dopaminergic pathways that originate from the VTA:

Mu opioid receptor: A type of opioid receptor that is present in GABA-ergic neurons and is central for the euphoric-inducing properties of opioids.

Ventral tegmental area (VTA): A group of neurons in the midbrain that contains a large number of dopaminergic cells and is the main structure from which dopaminergic axons project into the rest of the brain.

Dopamine: A neurotransmitter that plays a key role in the reward system of the brain.

- The mesocortical pathway from the VTA to the cortex: relevant for executive functions.
- The mesolimbic pathway from the VTA to the ventral striatum, the hippocampus, and the limbic system: relevant for reward-related wanting and liking.
- The nigrostriatal pathway from the VTA to the basal ganglia: relevant for motor function.

Nucleus accumbens: A component of the basal ganglia that is part of the reward network and crucial for the feeling of pleasure.

When fentanyl binds to the mu opioid receptor in GABAergic neurons, it quickly inhibits these cells. Because GABA normally inhibits dopamine, this process leads to a disinhibition of dopaminergic neurons in the mesolimbic pathway, which causes dopamine levels to rise in the **nucleus accumbens**, a part of the ventral striatum, which in turn is part of the basal ganglia (Chaudun et al., 2024). The nucleus accumbens plays a causal role in creating feelings of pleasure and euphoria, and the rapid increase of dopamine in the nucleus accumbens induced by fentanyl can explain the euphoria felt by many abusers. Thus, the mesolimbic pathway from the VTA to the ventral striatum is central for the acute euphoric effects of drugs. Although the exact neurochemical pathways differ between substance classes, the resulting increase of dopamine in the nucleus accumbens is what produces the experience of pleasure for most major drugs.

How powerful the stimulation of the mesolimbic dopaminergic pathway to the ventral striatum can be has been shown in a classic study using intracranial self-stimulation in rats (Olds & Milner, 1954). In this study, an electrode was implanted into the rat's brain to stimulate the dopaminergic pathways involved in reward. The animals were then placed in a box equipped with a lever linked to the energy generator of the electrode. As a result, the rats could stimulate their own reward system by pressing the lever, and they often did this for long periods of time instead of eating, drinking, or even sleeping.

Interestingly, dopamine not only plays a major role in the euphoria induced by drugs but also in the formation of romantic relationships and attraction to a partner (see Chapter 14 for details). The reward system responds to the experience of romantic love in a similar manner to how it reacts to addictive substances, although the rush is often less intense, making falling in love and using drugs somewhat similar processes on the neurochemical level (which may or may not explain why people sometimes act irrationally when being in love).

Substance addiction and withdrawal

Drug abusers often report that their first experience with a drug was the most pleasurable, and that the effects decreased over time, meaning they required larger quantities to achieve the same results. Psychobiological research has provided insight into the neural changes that turn drug use from being rewarding to an addiction (Volkow & Morales,

2015). First-time drug use is often a conscious choice (likely mediated by the prefrontal cortex) due to curiosity or the wish to feel euphoria. It leads to the aforementioned dopamine release in the nucleus accumbens. However, if the drug is used regularly, several neuroplastic changes (see Chapter 4) will take place in the brain. In general, repeated exposure will lead to a downregulation of dopamine receptors in the ventral striatum, which means that increasingly larger quantities of the drug are needed to achieve the same pleasurable effect. Other neuroplastic changes include a heightened reactivity of the brain to drug-related cues (such as seeing a glass pipe used to smoke fentanyl) and a reduced reactivity to non-drug cues, as well as reduced self-control and an increase in negative emotions. Over time, drug use becomes habitual, and reduced self-control turns drug-taking into a compulsive, automatic behaviour. With prolonged drug use, people often experience withdrawal symptoms when they go without the drug. These symptoms are driven by distinct brain networks from those that cause the initial pleasurable response to reflect more than just the absence of reward. For example, during fentanyl withdrawal, neurons expressing mu opioid receptors in the amygdala showed increased activity (Chaudun et al., 2024). As the amygdala is a core brain region for negative emotions, this may reflect psychological withdrawal symptoms, such as depression and anxiety, and may motivate repeated drug use to avoid these negative consequences.

Addicted to social media? The psychobiology of behavioural addictions

Classically, the focus of addiction research in clinical psychology is largely focused on **substance addiction,** such as alcohol or opioid painkillers. However, the reward system itself is indifferent to the rewarding stimulus, and in principle, any stimulus perceived as rewarding has the potential to become addictive. Such an addiction to a behaviour or the feeling induced by a behaviour is called **behavioural addiction** (Alavi et al., 2012). One of the most widely investigated forms of behavioural addiction is gambling, and gambling disorder is a recognised medical diagnosis. The neurobiological pathways are similar to those of drugs of abuse: during gambling, people with a gambling disorder show higher levels of dopamine in the mesolimbic system than controls. Several other

> **Substance addiction**: Addiction to a psychologically active substance such as alcohol or opioid painkillers.
>
> **Behavioural addiction:** Addiction to a behaviour or the feeling induced by a behaviour.

behavioural addictions that are investigated in psychological research include sex addiction, compulsive buying, internet addiction, video game addiction, and sports addiction. One type of behavioural addiction that has yet to be recognised with a medical diagnosis is social media use disorder (Moretta & Wegmann, 2025). A growing number of people report losing control over the time they spend on social media and experience impairments in their social life or jobs due to excessive consumption of social media content. Several studies have shown that social media use leads to activation of the brain's reward system and that receiving "likes" on social media platforms is a particularly rewarding experience for some users. Thus, while often not having severe consequences such as gambling or substance addictions, social media use does fulfil the prerequisites to be addictive and should be treated with caution, especially in children and adolescents.

Why do some people get addicted and others not?

Many people occasionally enjoy a pint of ale at a pub or smoke a cigarette once or twice without developing long-term alcohol or nicotine dependence. However, some go on to develop fully fledged alcohol or nicotine use disorders. Psychobiological research using genetic techniques (see Chapter 9) has contributed to a better understanding of why some people get addicted, and others do not. Overall, substance use disorders are highly heritable (up to 60%), indicating that not everyone has the same risk of developing a substance use disorder. People whose parents suffered from an addiction have a substantially higher chance of developing an addiction compared with those without a family history. In a genetic study with data from more than a million people, it was shown that the genetic basis of addiction is twofold (Hatoum et al., 2023). On the one hand, there were nineteen different genetic loci that affected general addiction risk independent of the abused substance. Functionally, these genes predominantly affected dopamine regulation, reflecting the fact that the mesolimbic dopamine system is the common final path of all addictions in the brain. In addition, there were further substance-specific genes that were predictive of the development of an addiction. These genes were functionally relevant for metabolic processes and receptors specifically relevant to different addictive substances. The substantial genetic risk in addiction questions whether drug use is a "choice" and highlights that biological vulnerability needs to be considered when understanding why someone gets addicted. In addition to these genetic factors, several environmental and individual factors have been shown to affect additional risk, including social influence of friends, social integration, being informed about the effects of drugs, and impulse control ability (Safari Hajat Aghaii et al., 2012). Thus, genes, environment, and development all affect psychobiological processes that determine why some people become addicted to drugs while others are not.

Conclusion

Addiction is a major societal issue across the whole world. Psychobiological research has highlighted the relevance of dopaminergic pathways in the brain's reward system in addiction, helping us understand the underlying neurobiology, which is ultimately important in informing long-term treatment. It can help in the development of pharmacological treatments for drug addiction, but also highlights the importance of taking genetic vulnerability factors into account, given the substantial genetic component of addiction.

Further reading

Additional academic source: Murphy, P. (2021). *Psychobiological Issues in Substance Use and Misuse.* Routledge.

Relevant web resource: "*Addiction: what is it?*" an info page on addiction by the National Health Service (NHS) in the UK. https://www.nhs.uk/live-well/addiction-support/addiction-what-is-it/

Related documentary: *Heroin(e)* (2017). A short documentary about how first responders in Huntington, West Virginia (USA), deal with an increasing number of overdoses due to the opioid crisis.

Related documentary: *Ten dollar death trip: Inside the fentanyl crisis* (2020). A documentary about the devastating effects that the synthetic opioid fentanyl has in public health in North America.

References

Alavi, S. S., Ferdosi, M., Jannatifard, F., Eslami, M., Alaghemandan, H., & Setare, M. (2012). Behavioral addiction versus substance addiction: correspondence of psychiatric and psychological views. *International Journal of Preventive Medicine, 3*, 290–294.

Chaudun, F., Python, L., Liu, Y., Hiver, A., Cand, J., Kieffer, B. L., Valjent, E., & Lüscher, C. (2024). Distinct μ-opioid ensembles trigger positive and negative fentanyl reinforcement. *Nature, 630*, 141–148. https://doi.org/10.1038/s41586-024-07440-x

Hatoum, A. S., Colbert, S. M. C., Johnson, E. C., Huggett, S. B., Deak, J. D., Pathak, G., Jennings, M. V., Paul, S. E., Karcher, N. R., Hansen, I., Baranger, D. A. A., Edwards, A., Grotzinger, A., Substance Use Disorder Working Group of the Psychiatric Genomics Consortium, Tucker-Drob, E. M., Kranzler, H. R., Davis, L. K., Sanchez-Roige, S., Polimanti, R., … Agrawal, A. (2023). Multivariate genome-wide association meta-analysis of over 1 million subjects identifies loci underlying multiple substance use disorders. *Nature Mental Health*, *1*, 210–223. https://doi.org/10.1038/s44220-023-00034-y

Moretta, T., & Wegmann, E. (2025). Toward the classification of social media use disorder: clinical characterization and proposed diagnostic criteria. *Addictive Behaviors Reports*, *21*, 100603. https://doi.org/10.1016/j.abrep.2025.100603

National Center for Health Statistics. (2025). *U.S. Overdose Deaths Decrease Almost 27% in 2024.* National Center for Health Statistics. Retrieved 15 August 2025 from https://www.cdc.gov/nchs/pressroom/releases/20250514.html

Olds, J., & Milner, P. (1954). Positive reinforcement produced by electrical stimulation of septal area and other regions of rat brain. *Journal of Comparative and Physiological Psychology*, *47*, 419–427. https://doi.org/10.1037/h0058775

Safari Hajat Aghaii, S., Kamaly, A., & Esfahani, M. (2012). Meta-analysis of individual and environmental factors that influence people's addiction tendencies. *International Journal of High Risk Behaviors & Addiction*, *1*, 92–99. https://doi.org/10.5812/ijhrba.5330

Volkow, N. D., & Morales, M. (2015). The brain on drugs: from reward to addiction. *Cell*, *162*, 712–725. https://doi.org/10.1016/j.cell.2015.07.046

Chapter 14

Hug me until I stop crying

Psychobiological research on social and emotional processes

Introduction

As a natural science, psychobiology aims to understand the biological processes that drive behaviour and cognition. This usually involves identifying general principles of how the brain or nervous system works in all humans. For example, the action potential in neuron-to-neuron communication will follow the same rules in everyone. However, some psychological processes are highly individualistic and not easily comparable across individuals. One such example is romantic love, a phenomenon crucial for the mental well-being (or not being so well) of many (but not all) people. Sometimes, we meet someone new, and they quickly become the most important person in the world to us. Understanding what happens in the brain and body in this highly individual and complex situation is a great challenge for psychobiology. The same is true for other social bonds such as friendships and parental relationships. While psychobiological research cannot solve these mysteries alone, it has made tremendous advances in the last few decades in understanding the neuronal and hormonal processes underlying social bonds and interpersonal emotions that shape our lives.

The psychobiology of love: dopamine and oxytocin

Sometimes, life can change in an instant: we meet that one special person, and being around them feels so different, breath-taking, and euphoric that nothing else in the world compares. Being in love with someone can be one of life's greatest joys, but it can also bring anguish and unbearable pain if the other person does not feel the same. What happens in the brain when we experience intense emotions like these? Scientists have made great progress in understanding the psychobiology of romantic love using neuroimaging and other methods, as well as measurements of hormones and other substances in the brain and body. They have revealed that the brain's reward

DOI: 10.4324/9781003571537-18

Dopamine: A neurotransmitter that plays a key role in the reward system of the brain. The anticipation of a reward increases the dopamine levels in brain structures within the reward system.

Oxytocin: A hormone that is produced in the hypothalamus. It plays a key role in social bonding of humans and animals.

Vasopressin: A hormone that is produced in the hypothalamus. It plays a role in kidney function, but it is also important for social bonding. It is structurally very similar to oxytocin.

system and psychobiological bonding processes are crucial for establishing and maintaining love, with the neurotransmitter **dopamine** and the hormones **oxytocin** and **vasopressin** being key players (Zeki, 2007).

Different research groups have used functional magnetic resonance imaging (fMRI) (see Chapter 8) to assess what happens in the brain when people look at pictures of someone they love or think romantic thoughts about a person. Most prominently, these studies have shown that areas involved in the brain's reward system are activated, like the ventral tegmental area and the caudate nucleus. Dopamine is the central neurotransmitter in the reward system. Being in love leads to the release of dopamine in this system, which is associated with feelings of desire, wanting, and euphoria. Interestingly, dopaminergic receptors in the reward system are also activated by many other types of rewards, such as certain euphoria-inducing drugs like cocaine. Thus, neurobiologically, the euphoria of being in love is similar to a drug-induced high. While dopamine levels in the reward system rise, serotonin, a neurotransmitter associated with mood and appetite for food, gets depleted. Low levels of serotonin have also been observed in patients with obsessive–compulsive disorder, which may explain why someone in love often obsessively thinks about the person they love and engages in compulsive, sometimes risky behaviours to gain their attention.

While the dopamine system is central in the early stages of passionate romantic love, it is not the only system relevant to long-term relationships. Many couples (sadly) find that the intense euphoria they experience in the early weeks of a newly formed relationship fades over time. This may be because dopamine does not encode the reward value itself but the so-called reward prediction error. This means that the difference between the expected reward and the reward obtained is crucial for the dopamine response. Everything is new and surprising at the beginning of a relationship, which is why the first kiss feels much more special than the 10,000th kiss for many couples. Importantly, the dopamine response alone does not keep couples together in happy, long-lasting relationships. Long-term emotional attachment and bonding are commonly associated with two structurally very similar hormones: oxytocin and vasopressin. Both hormones are produced by the pituitary gland in the hypothalamus, a brain area that is an important link between the nervous system and hormonal systems. Oxytocin has several important functions in the body, including uterine contraction during birth and the milk ejection reflex in breastfeeding mothers. Oxytocin levels rise during sexual activity and orgasm, but also increase with social touch. The oxytocin released during intimate interaction with another person is central to forming long-lasting pair bonds. Oxytocin also directly interacts with the reward system. For example, an fMRI study in which heterosexual men used a nasal spray containing oxytocin showed that oxytocin enhanced activation in the brain's reward system when the men viewed pictures of their female partners, compared to men not given oxytocin (Scheele et al., 2013). Understanding the molecular factors relevant to love and other forms of social bonding is also highly relevant to understanding what happens when an important social relationship is lost forever. For example, researchers have proposed that when a romantic relationship ends, the loss of a major social bond disrupts oxytocin signalling, leading to emotional problems and a higher risk for mental health issues (Hurlemann & Scheele, 2016). This may explain why the death of a partner or the end of a romantic relationship can feel so devastating, as well as why ghosting, a recent toxic dating trend in which somebody suddenly ends all communication with a dating partner without warning, can lead to severe negative feelings.

The psychobiology of social touch

While much psychological research on communication is focused on speaking (after all, therapists speak with their patients during their sessions), non-verbal communication via touch is a major focus of social neuroscience. Touch is one of the earliest forms of social communication. For example, if a parent wants to calm a crying baby, they cannot talk to the baby but can use cradling to comfort it and make it feel better. Similarly, adults use several forms of social touch to communicate happiness or love, or to calm someone down when they are stressed or sad. Figure 14.1 shows kissing, hugging, and cradling, three major forms of social touch.

Interestingly, the same form of social touch can be used in both emotionally positive situations (such as hugging the bride or groom at a wedding to congratulate them) and emotionally negative situations (such as hugging someone at a funeral after their partner passed away). From a psychobiological perspective, social touch is detected by two types of

Figure 14.1 Three major forms of social touch in humans are kissing, hugging, and cradling.

receptor cells in the skin: one type of receptor that responds to gentle stroking, and another type of receptor that responds to deep pressure. Social touch leads to the release of both oxytocin and dopamine, which subsequently activate brain regions associated with positive emotions.

The psychobiology of loneliness

Having meaningful social connections is an important part of life, but what happens in the brain and body when someone feels lonely? Loneliness is not the same as being alone. It generally describes a feeling that one lacks meaningful social relationships. Feelings of loneliness can also occur when people have a lot of superficial relationships but feel that these relationships lack in quality and emotional depth. According to the Campaign to End Loneliness (2024), loneliness is a major societal issue in the UK, with about 50% of adults feeling lonely sometimes and 3.83 million people experiencing chronic loneliness. These numbers showed a particularly sharp increase during the COVID-19 pandemic. This epidemic of loneliness is a societal issue for the UK and other societies, especially since chronic loneliness is associated with decreased life expectancy. Psychobiological research can contribute to a better understanding of how loneliness affects the body and the brain in our efforts to combat these issues. A study on loneliness and the social brain (Lieberz et al., 2021) found that people who feel very lonely have a reduced oxytocin response and experience fewer positive emotions during a nice conversation with another person. They also showed less trust in other people and preferred to stand further away from another person. Using fMRI, researchers also found that, compared to people with satisfying social relationships, severely lonely individuals showed changes in both the limbic system, relevant to emotion, and the reward system of the brain. Additionally, they showed reduced connections between brain areas relevant to positive emotions. These findings highlight that loneliness has a profound impact on both hormonal and brain systems associated with social bonding.

The psychobiology of emotions

An important topic in psychobiological research that is often linked to social situations is the neuroscientific investigation of emotions. Emotions are mental states that involve a subjective feeling (such as fear), a tendency to act in a certain way (such as running away from an aggressive dog), physiological changes in the central and peripheral nervous systems, as well as in hormonal systems (such as activation of the **amygdala** and release of stress hormones). Social situations can elicit many different positive emotions, such as happiness when spending time with a loved one, or negative emotions like fear when faced with an unpleasant situation, such as being interrogated by the police. Emotions can, of course, also happen outside of social interactions, such as when someone sits alone in their room and feels intense sadness for being left by their partner. At their most basic level, emotions can elicit two different tendencies to act: approach (such as going towards a nice person) and avoidance (such as running away from an angry grizzly bear). On the brain level, emotions such as happiness, surprise, fear, aggression, and disgust are produced in the **limbic system** (from "limbus", Latin for "border" as several brain areas in the limbic system form the border between the cortex and the brain stem). The limbic system is a complex (and rather loosely defined) network of brain areas such as the amygdala, the hippocampus, the hypothalamus, the fornix, the orbitofrontal cortex, and other brain areas. The central component in the limbic system is the amygdala, which is located medially in the temporal lobe. It consists of several nuclei and plays a key role in emotional responses, especially for fear and aggression. Other key structures for emotions include the hypothalamus (relevant for the physiological emotion response, such as crying), the hippocampus (relevant

Amygdala: The amygdala is a central component in the limbic system and is located medially in the temporal lobe. It consists of several nuclei and plays a key role in emotional responses, especially for fear and aggression.

Limbic system: A network of brain areas relevant to emotion. It contains the amygdala, the hippocampus, the hypothalamus, the fornix, the orbitofrontal cortex, and other brain areas.

for emotional memories), and the anterior cingulate cortex (relevant for conscious feeling of emotions). Moreover, the prefrontal cortex (relevant for regulating emotions) and the ventral striatum (relevant for the reward component of positive emotions) are key players in affective processes.

Investigating cognitive social processes

In addition to investigating socio-affective processes, psychobiological research has contributed to a better understanding of cognitive processes related to understanding social interactions. Interacting with other people is not purely a social or emotional process but often involves continued thinking and decision-making about how to interact with the other person. Research on cognitive social process includes, for example, fMRI research on the psychobiological basis of having a **theory of mind**, the process of gaining insights about the mental states of other people. Using different theory of mind paradigms, scientists could show that a fronto-temporal network of brain areas involved in emotion processing, stimulus categorisation, and executive functions is relevant for having a theory of mind. Another cognitive social process that has been investigated using fMRI is moral reasoning (what people think is right or wrong).

Many of the experiments described in the previous section tested only one person at a time, like almost all studies in psychobiology. This methodology may limit the insights into social neuroscience, as social situations, by definition, include two people. To combat this issue, a psychobiological technique called **hyperscanning** was developed (Czeszumski et al., 2020). In a nutshell, hyperscanning involves simultaneously recording psychobiological data from two or more participants at the same time, using methods such as fMRI, electroencephalogram (EEG), magnetoencephalogram, or functional near-infrared spectroscopy. Using specialised statistical analyses, the data from the participants are then analysed together to gain insights about their association. Figure 14.2 shows EEG hyperscanning, the most common form of hyperscanning. EEG is particularly well-suited for hyperscanning in social neuroscience due to the high temporal resolution that allows it to capture fast neuronal processes

Theory of mind: The process of gaining insights about the mental states of other people.

Hyperscanning: Measure the brain activity of more than one participant simultaneously using methods like EEG or fMRI.

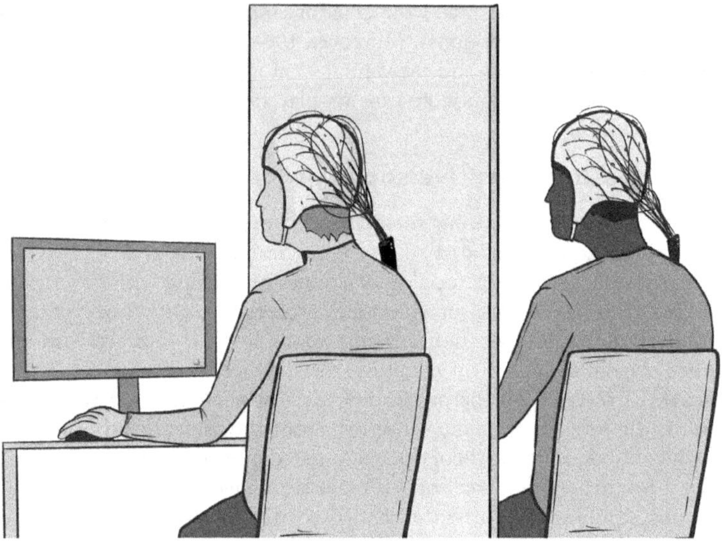

Figure 14.2 EEG hyperscanning. Two participants perform an interactive experimental task while an EEG signals are recorded from both individuals.

well that may be highly relevant in interactive tasks. It can, for example, be used for hyperscanning during kissing or hugging.

Conclusion

Social and emotional processes are an important part of life, and psychobiological research can contribute to a better understanding of them. Most importantly, it is central in generating the necessary knowledge to combat major societal challenges, like the epidemic of loneliness, by providing empirical insights on the neuronal and hormonal bases of social and emotional processes.

Further reading

Additional academic source: Harmon-Jones, E., & Inzlicht, M. (Eds.). (2016). *Social Neuroscience Biological Approaches to Social Psychology*. Routledge.

Relevant web resource: The BPS website on relationships offers many fascinating insights into psychological research on social bonds: https://www.bps.org.uk/collections/relationships-love-and-sex

References

Campaign to End Loneliness. (2024). Facts and statistics about loneliness. Retrieved 17 February 2025 from https://www.campaigntoendloneliness.org/facts-and-statistics/

Czeszumski, A., Eustergerling, S., Lang, A., Menrath, D., Gerstenberger, M., Schuberth, S., Schreiber, F., Rendon, Z. Z., & König, P. (2020). Hyperscanning: a valid method to study neural inter-brain underpinnings of social interaction. *Frontiers in Human Neuroscience, 14,* 39. https://doi.org/10.3389/fnhum.2020.00039

Hurlemann, R., & Scheele, D. (2016). Dissecting the role of oxytocin in the formation and loss of social relationships. *Biological Psychiatry, 79*, 185–193. https://doi.org/10.1016/j.biopsych.2015.05.013

Lieberz, J., Shamay-Tsoory, S. G., Saporta, N., Esser, T., Kuskova, E., Stoffel-Wagner, B., Hurlemann, R., & Scheele, D. (2021). Loneliness and the social brain: how perceived social isolation impairs human interactions. *Advanced Science, 8*, e2102076. https://doi.org/10.1002/advs.202102076

Scheele, D., Wille, A., Kendrick, K. M., Stoffel-Wagner, B., Becker, B., Güntürkün, O., Maier, W., & Hurlemann, R. (2013). Oxytocin enhances brain reward system responses in men viewing the face of their female partner. *Proceedings of the National Academy of Sciences of the United States of America, 110*, 20308–20313. https://doi.org/10.1073/pnas.1314190110

Zeki, S. (2007). The neurobiology of love. *FEBS Letters, 581*, 2575–2579. https://doi.org/10.1016/j.febslet.2007.03.094

Chapter 15

Not hungry, anymore

The psychobiology of hunger in the age of weight-loss pills

Introduction

We all need to eat to survive. Yet, eating too much and not eating enough are both at the heart of many societal struggles and psychiatric disorders. Obesity has become a major health issue worldwide, and recent surveys estimate that 60% of UK adults are overweight and around one-fourth live with obesity. The World Health Organization (2025) defines obesity as abnormal or excessive fat accumulation that presents a risk to health. These health risks include type two diabetes, heart disease, stroke, certain cancers, as well as liver and kidney conditions. It also shortens life expectancy and can significantly reduce the quality of life. However, obesity is more than a medical condition; it is wrapped up in **stigma,** negative attitudes, beliefs, or behaviours directed towards a group of people, and unrealistic societal expectations. Negative attitudes towards people with obesity are widespread in media, medical settings, and from the public, often blaming the individual (Baker et al., 2020; Flint et al., 2015). Social media amplifies individual pressures as they overflow with digitally modified, unrealistically thin bodies, encouraging users to measure themselves against these unrealistic ideals. The platforms are aware that this is a problem and sometimes intervene, such as in 2025 when the hashtag #skinnytok, promoting extreme thinness, was banned on a popular platform. The infamous quote "*nothing tastes as good as skinny feels*" exemplifies the promotion of extreme thinness and unhealthy body ideals. The disconnect between reality and what society demands can encourage self-doubt and harmful comparisons in the healthiest of individuals and lead to distorted eating behaviours that contribute to both obesity and eating disorders.

> **Stigma:** Negative attitudes, beliefs, or behaviours about or towards a group of people.

DOI: 10.4324/9781003571537-19

Psychobiological mechanisms of hunger

Hunger is a biological sensation that reminds us that our body needs nutrients in the form of food. Hunger and eating might seem like the simplest and most natural things in the world: you have an empty stomach, so you eat. In reality, appetite is far more complex. It is shaped not only by biological need but also by psychological processes and our environment. Imagine going to your favourite restaurant. You just enjoyed a delicious meal, and you feel full and satisfied. Then, the server brings out the dessert menu. Although you are already full, you still have some room for that heavenly slice of chocolate cake that makes your mouth water just by thinking of it. Scientists tend to distinguish between two types of hunger: **homeostatic hunger**, which drives us to eat when our bodies need energy, and **hedonic hunger**, which is when we eat for pleasure, even when not necessarily physically hungry.

Homeostatic hunger

Homeostatic hunger is thought to be regulated by a balance between energy intake and expenditure. Historically, this homeostatic control helped humans store energy during times of abundance and conserve it when food was scarce. This type of hunger is regulated by short-term and long-term signals that generate the feeling of hunger when energy stores are low and suppress it when energy needs are met. These signals help control when, what, and how much we eat. Long-term (tonic) signals are influences on hunger and appetite that remain relatively stable over the day. This includes the hormone leptin, which is produced from body fat. Leptin levels in the blood are proportionate to the amount of body fat a person has. Leptin will travel to the brain and bind to receptors in the hypothalamus and brain stem. The activation of these areas will lead to various changes related to appetite control. Leptin levels also play a role in the body's **metabolism**, the chemical reactions in cells that convert food into energy. The body can become leptin-resistant, meaning the brain stops responding to signals that enough energy is stored. This has been found to create constant feelings of hunger and a reduced metabolism and

> **Homeostatic hunger:** Eating that is regulated by energy balance and physiological need.
>
> **Hedonic hunger:** Eating that is driven by pleasure and not energy need.
>
> **Metabolism:** The chemical reactions in cells that convert food into energy.

Ghrelin: A hormone that stimulates appetite and signals the brain to increase food intake. The "hunger hormone".

can result in a weight gain cycle, as it can lead to overeating while calories burned are reduced.

Short-term (episodic) signals are temporary changes that occur during the day in response to food intake. Brain circuits that include the hypothalamus help detect these signals and regulate how the body responds. These signals mostly arrive from the gastrointestinal (GI) tract, which contains all the major organs of the digestive system. When the stomach is mostly empty, it secretes the hormone **ghrelin**, often called the "hunger hormone", which is mainly produced in the stomach. Ghrelin travels to the hypothalamus and activates specific neurons called agouti-related peptide neurons, which increase appetite. In addition, the GI tract also sends messages to the brain through the vagus nerve, which triggers dopamine release that reinforces feelings of hunger and promotes food-seeking behaviour. Besides ghrelin, hunger can also be increased from low blood sugar (hypoglycaemia) and muscle contractions in the stomach called motilin-induced phase III contractions that signal to the brain that it is time to eat.

When we eat, the body will initiate a set of signals to quickly turn off hunger. Sensors in the stomach will pick up on the presence of food and signal the brain. The presence of nutrients, such as amino acids and fats, strengthens these satiety signals. In addition, digested food in the small intestine triggers the secretion of several GI hormones, such as glucagon-like peptide one (GLP-1), cholecystokinin (CCK), and peptide YY (PYY). CCK signals the brain through the vagus nerve to promote fullness and digestion. The lower intestine releases PYY, which reduces appetite and slows how quickly food leaves the stomach. GLP-1 helps people feel full longer, lowers appetite, and controls blood sugar by increasing insulin release.

Hedonic hunger

If hunger and eating behaviour were controlled strictly by homeostasis, we would not struggle with overeating. Homeostasis alone also fails to explain why we instinctively reach for pizza instead of a salad, or why we indulge in dessert even when full. Hedonic, or pleasure-driven, hunger reflects the desire to eat for enjoyment, even when the body does not need energy. Brain reward pathways play a central role in regulating eating, but these are also influenced by environmental cues and learned behaviours that can influence eating behaviour. For example, a classic study by Stice et al. (2008) used functional magnetic resonance imaging (fMRI) to examine the brain's response to both the anticipation and the consumption of chocolate milkshakes. They showed that reward-related brain regions were activated both by anticipation and actual consumption of palatable foods. This suggests that the expectation of pleasure can be a very important factor in driving eating behaviour. This has also been supported by research demonstrating that heightened activity in food-related reward circuits increases the risk of future weight gain, potentially explaining why some individuals seek out pleasurable foods more readily. Thus, pleasure-driven signals from the brain can override hunger and fullness cues, making you order that extra piece of chocolate cake. Learned associations, exposure to food cues, and social contexts can all stimulate the brain's reward system. Other situational factors, such as stress and negative emotions, affect eating in different ways: for some people, they increase hunger and make tasty foods more appealing, while for others, they suppress appetite and reduce eating behaviour.

Drug therapies for weight management

Recently, weight-management medications have made headlines, in large part thanks to endorsements from celebrities and social media influencers. These stories have dominated tabloids and social media feeds, creating a perception that "quick fixes" are both glamorous and accessible. Despite all the media hype, long-term weight loss is still a major challenge. Many drugs and weight-loss pills have been tried to target these processes, but their success has been mixed. Several of the newer weight-management medications are GLP-1 receptor agonists, drugs that mimic a natural hormone by binding to their specific receptors and triggering the same responses. GLP-1 drugs were originally developed to treat diabetes because they stimulate insulin and lower blood sugar (Kreymann et al., 1987), but were subsequently found to cause significant weight loss in the people who took them. Today, it is the most widely used category of weight-loss medications. GLP-1 receptor agonists function by acting on both the gut and the brain. These are sometimes combined with other receptor agonists (called dual agonists), such as GLP-1 with glucose-dependent insulinotropic polypeptide (GIP) or insulin-like growth factor. GLP-1 and GIP support weight loss by reducing hunger, slowing food intake, and enhancing the feeling of satiety. GLP-1 activates receptors in the hypothalamus, brainstem, and gut, triggering multiple effects: it increases insulin release, lowers glucagon, slows gastric emptying via the vagus nerve, and activates satiety-promoting neurons while inhibiting hunger neurons. GIP stimulates insulin secretion and works alongside GLP-1 to enhance the treatment's overall effectiveness. GLP-1 also interacts with other hormonal signals involved in appetite regulation, including PYY, CCK, insulin, and leptin, which together regulate neural circuits controlling feeding behaviour. In addition, GLP-1 acts on brain regions involved in reward and memory, including the hippocampus, ventral tegmental area, and nucleus accumbens. Through its action on the mesolimbic reward pathway (see Chapter 13), it can change how we experience motivation, pleasure, and emotion in response to food. This effect has prompted research into GLP-1 drugs for addiction, as they have the potential to reduce dopamine release, decreasing the rewarding effects of substances like alcohol.

Unfortunately, these medications only work while they are taken. Once treatment stops, the body's hunger, satiety, and energy balance return to baseline, and many people regain the lost weight within 1.5–2 years (West et al., 2026), often at a faster rate than after stopping behavioural weight-loss programmes based on diet and exercise. This likely reflects the difference in approaches: drugs mainly affect hunger and reward systems, while behavioural programmes promote practical strategies and healthy habits that result in long-term behaviour change.

Disordered eating

Eating disorders are serious psychiatric disorders marked by severe disturbances in a person's eating behaviours. The most common being anorexia nervosa (AN), bulimia nervosa, and binge eating disorder. For example, **AN** is an eating disorder where a person intentionally restricts food intake, often leading to dangerously low body weight. Eating disorders in the UK are on the rise due to a mix of societal pressures, including social media and body image ideals, psychological vulnerabilities such as anxiety and perfectionism, and biological risk factors. Pandemic-related stress and online influences like pro-eating disorder ("pro-ana") content have also contributed, especially in young people. Because eating disorders can arise for many different reasons, they are very difficult to treat.

Research from large twin studies highlights how significantly genetics influence eating disorders. For example, in cases of AN, heritability can be as high as 0.74, indicating that nearly 75% of the differences in risk are due to genetic factors (Bulik et al., 2022). Our understanding of the psychobiology behind eating disorders is continually growing, but it can be challenging to distinguish cause from effect. This is because brain differences observed in people with eating disorders may sometimes be a result of the disorder itself. For instance, studies consistently show

Anorexia nervosa (AN): An eating disorder where a person intentionally restricts food intake, often leading to dangerously low body weight.

reduced grey matter volume in individuals with AN, but this might reflect the disease state, as some researchers do not find these differences after recovery. On the other hand, fMRI points to altered brain activity in reward and emotional areas. In particular, people with AN tend to have weaker responses in reward-related brain regions when viewing tasty foods, but increased activity in emotion-related areas such as the amygdala and bodily awareness-related regions like the insula. This suggests that their brains may process reward and fear differently. One study looked at how people with AN process food-related images and emotional pictures, comparing adolescents and adults (Horndasch et al., 2018). They found that adolescents with AN, in particular, showed stronger activity in brain regions associated with emotion, reward, and self-control when viewing high-calorie foods. This indicates that especially teenagers with AN tend to have more intense emotional and control-related responses to food stimuli. Overall, these brain imaging studies help us see how altered brain circuits involved in reward and self-control are linked to eating disorders, which can provide valuable insight into how to treat them.

Conclusion

Psychobiological insights into hunger and food-seeking behaviour can help us understand biological signals and psychological and environmental factors that play a role in eating behaviour. Recognising the interplay between the brain, hormones, and external factors helps us better understand why individuals may struggle with disordered eating. Using these insights, we can develop more effective strategies for promoting healthy eating behaviours, reducing stigma surrounding disordered eating, and supporting long-term well-being in the population.

Further reading

Related documentary: Food on the Brain (BBC, 2015). Focuses on how the brain regulates hunger, satiety, and cravings, connecting neuroscience to eating behaviour.

Related podcast: Fat Science, https://fatsciencepodcast.com/, a podcast on a mission to provide accurate information about metabolism and recognise that fat is not a failure.

Related podcast: Maintenance Phase, https://www.maintenancephase.com/, a health science and pop culture podcast that aims to debunk health and wellness-industry myths.

Relevant web source: Psychological perspectives on obesity: *Addressing policy, practice and research priorities* (2019). The British Psychological Society, https://explore.bps.org.uk/content/report-guideline/bpsrep.2019.rep130/ https://doi.org/10.53841/bpsrep.2019.rep130

References

Baker, P., Brookes, G., Atanasova, D., & Flint, S. W. (2020). Changing frames of obesity in the UK press 2008–2017. *Social Science & Medicine*, *264*, 113403. https://doi.org/10.1016/j.socscimed.2020.113403

Bulik, C. M., Coleman, J. R., Hardaway, J. A., Breithaupt, L., Watson, H. J., Bryant, C. D., & Breen, G. (2022). Genetics and neurobiology of eating disorders. *Nature Neuroscience*, *25*(5), 543–554. https://doi.org/10.1038/s41593-022-01071-z

Flint, S. W., Hudson, J., & Lavallee, D. (2015). UK adults' implicit and explicit attitudes towards obesity: a cross-sectional study. *BMC Obesity*, *2*(1), 31. https://doi.org/10.1186/s40608-015-0064-2

Horndasch, S., Roesch, J., Forster, C., Dörfler, A., Lindsiepe, S., Heinrich, H., Graap, H., Moll, G. H., & Kratz, O. (2018). Neural processing of food and emotional stimuli in adolescent and adult anorexia nervosa patients. *PLoS One*, *13*(3), e0191059. https://doi.org/10.1371/journal.pone.0191059

Kreymann, B., Ghatei, M. A., Williams, G., & Bloom, S. R. (1987). Glucagon-like peptide-1 7–36: a physiological incretin in man. *The Lancet*, *330*(8571), 1300–1304. https://doi.org/10.1016/s0140-6736(87)91194-9

Stice, E., Spoor, S., Bohon, C., Veldhuizen, M. G., & Small, D. M. (2008). Relation of reward from food intake and anticipated food intake to obesity: a functional magnetic resonance imaging study. *Journal of Abnormal Psychology*, *117*(4), 924–935. https://doi.org/10.1037/a0013600

West, S., Scragg, J., Aveyard, P., Oke, J. L., Willis, L., Haffner, S. J., Knight, H., Wang, D., Morrow, S., Heath, L., Jebb, S. A., & Koutoukidis, D. A. (2026). Weight regain after cessation of medication for weight management: systematic review and meta-analysis. *BMJ*, *392*. https://doi.org/10.1136/bmj-2025-085304

World Health Organization. (2025, December). *Obesity and Overweight*. World Health Organization https://www.who.int/news-room/fact-sheets/detail/obesity-and-overweight

Chapter 16

The self-conscious dolphin

What psychobiology can teach us about animal brains

Introduction

Like most scientists interested in psychological research questions, psychobiologists mostly conduct research on human volunteers. However, psychobiological research is not only limited to humans but has also been conducted in many animal species. Many of the methods described in previous chapters can also be applied to non-human animals. For example, a recent study used functional magnetic resonance imaging (fMRI) to noninvasively map how the dog brain responds to touch (Guran et al., 2024). To do so, dogs were first extensively trained in the scanner environment and using the touch task, and dog owners provided consent for their pets to participate in the study. On the day of data collection, the dogs walked into the scanner on their own and were awake and unrestrained during the entire scan. Using this approach, the scientists identified touch-sensitive brain areas in awake dogs without causing harm or stress, and illustrated that fMRI can be a useful tool in understanding animal brains. In addition to dogs, this fMRI has been used in many other species, including rats, mice, apes, monkeys, and even pigeons and songbirds. Similarly, other psychobiological techniques such as electroencephalogram (EEG), genetic methods, and hormonal measurements (e.g., of stress hormones) can be used in animals. In this chapter, we will provide examples of psychobiological research in animals and discuss the insights it has yielded.

Consciousness: a big question in psychobiological research

One of the biggest questions in psychobiological research in non-human animals is whether they can, in principle, show **consciousness,** and if so, which species do so. Consciousness is a term that has been defined in many ways, but it generally refers to a subjective awareness and experience of one's body and the surrounding world. In humans, consciousness can be

DOI: 10.4324/9781003571537-20

> **Consciousness**: Subjective awareness and experience of one's body and the surrounding world.
>
> **Mirror self-recognition (MSR):** The ability to recognise oneself in the mirror. It is assessed in the MSR test to determine the visual self-awareness of an animal.

assessed relatively easily by asking individuals about their experiences. For animals, however, this approach is impossible since they do not speak. How, then, can we assess consciousness in animals? This is a tough question, but scientists have come up with several great ideas. As consciousness is a complex construct, researchers have suggested breaking it down and examining its different aspects in animals to make it easier to create meaningful psychobiological experiments. One recent approach identified five different dimensions of animal consciousness (Birch et al., 2020). These included:

1 **Perceptual richness**: Does the animal perceive its environment with a high level of detail? This can be assessed using perceptual tests such as colour discrimination or olfactory discrimination tests.
2 **Evaluative richness**: Does the animal evaluate its environment with a wide range of different emotions? This can be assessed by designing tests focused on positive and negative emotions.
3 **Integration at a time**: Does the animal have a unified experience of itself at any given time point? This can be tested by assessing the neuroanatomy of an animal (e.g., does it have connections between its brain hemispheres that allow for a unified experience across the two halves of the brain) and by tasks in which information from different sources needs to be integrated.
4 **Integration across time**: Does the animal have the experience of a constant flow of moments across time? This can be assessed by experiments that need the retrieval of memories of past events or planning for future events.
5 **Self-consciousness**: Does the animal have a conscious awareness of itself distinct from other animals and its environment? This can, for example, be assessed using mirror self-recognition (see below).

The fifth point, in particular, has been extensively investigated in psychobiological research. One way to determine whether an animal has visual self-awareness is the **mirror self-recognition (MSR) test** (Murray et al., 2022). In this test, a mark (e.g., a brightly coloured dot) is placed on the animal (e.g., spray-painted or glued on the animal). The animal is then placed in front of a mirror, and the scientists observe to what extent the animal interacts with the dot. This is often compared to a control condition in which no mirror is present. If the animal spends significantly more time interacting with the dot (e.g., trying to scrape it off with its paws) in the mirror condition compared to the control condition, it is assumed that it can recognise itself in the mirror and attempts to remove the dot, as it does not belong to its body. When the animal ignores its mirror image or even attacks, it does not pass the MSR test. Figure 16.1 shows an example of the MRS test in a dog.

Human children typically pass the MSR test around the age of two. Several different animal species, including chimpanzees, bottlenose dolphins, Asian elephants, and magpies, have also been shown to pass the MRS test (Birch et al., 2020), suggesting these species, like humans, demonstrate visual self-awareness. However, one important scientific question is to what extent not passing the MSR test indicates that the

Figure 16.1 An example of the mirror self-recognition test in a dog.

animal does not have visual self-awareness. It has been suggested that the test often produces false negative results if it is not optimised for the typical behavioural repertoire of a species. One example of this is a recent study on MSR in chickens, the most eaten type of poultry in the world (Hillemacher et al., 2023). The scientists utilised a species-typical behaviour in the experiment: the warning call of roosters. Chickens are often attacked by aerial predators like hawks or eagles. When in a larger group, a rooster that spots a predatory bird flying overhead will emit a loud warning call, allowing the other chickens to flee and take cover under trees or bushes. This warning call, however, comes with a risk to the rooster, as it may attract the attention of the predatory bird and increase the risk of getting attacked. Thus, it comes as no surprise that roosters do not emit a warning call if they spot a predatory bird when they are alone. In the experiment, roosters were either placed alone, with another male, or with a mirror, while the silhouette of a hawk flew above them. As expected, they emitted a warning call when placed with another animal but not when they were alone. But what happened in the crucial mirror condition? Here, they did not emit a warning call, suggesting that they were aware the animal in the mirror was their own reflection and not a different rooster. Thus, although roosters fail the classic MSR test, this finding suggests that they show visual self-awareness if measured in a way that aligns with their natural behaviour. The finding also has important implications that need to be considered regarding animal welfare. As the most widely consumed bird species in the world, chickens are often bred and housed under industrial conditions. The finding that they show self-awareness suggests that they may have far more complex minds than previously assumed, and we need to take this into account when addressing animal welfare.

The tail-wagging dog: animal emotions

Humans show a wide range of emotions such as fear, surprise, happiness, anger, and disgust. Many animals show similar emotions, which are often evident from their behaviour. For example, a dog can become anxious if it spots a larger, dominant, and aggressive dog, consequently causing it to retreat and avoid the other dog. Or it can happily wiggle its tail and run towards its owner when they come home after work, and so on. These behavioural observations of emotions are further backed by psychobiological findings on brain anatomy. For example, the amygdala in the medial temporal lobe is one of the core structures of the human brain for emotional responses, such as fear, anxiety, and aggression. The amygdala is a phylogenetically old, highly evolutionarily conserved brain structure that is present in the brains of all vertebrate animals. This indicates that on the neuronal level, all vertebrates have the basic neuroanatomy required to experience emotions. It is, however, not trivial to determine whether specific emotions are present in different animal species. While some of the basic emotions, such as fear and aggression, are found in many species, more complex emotions may require more complex brains and may therefore not be present in all species. For example, it is known that monkeys can feel jealousy if another animal gets a better food reward, but we do not know whether hedgehogs or goats feel jealousy.

One experimental way to find out about animal emotions is based on the concept of hemispheric asymmetries in emotions: the idea that the left hemisphere of the brain is more relevant for positive emotions and the right hemisphere more relevant for negative emotions. In a study in dogs, high-speed cameras were used to analyse tail-wagging responses to either their owner (a positive stimulus for the dogs) or an unfamiliar dominant dog (a negative stimulus for the dogs) (Quaranta et al., 2007). When seeing their owner, dogs showed a strong rightward bias of tail-wagging, suggesting stronger motor control of the left hemisphere, which is associated with positive emotions. On the contrary, seeing the dominant dog elicited a leftward bias in tail-wagging, suggesting stronger motor control of the right hemisphere associated with negative emotions. Thus, observing tail wagging presents a non-invasive method to assess both positive and negative emotions in dogs.

Cognition without cortex: the amazing bird brain

"Bird brain" is a term sometimes used to describe someone stupid. This insult resulted from the long-held misconception that birds have small, primitive brains that prevent them from showing complex intelligent behaviour. In addition, birds do not have a six-layered neocortex that makes up about 90% of the cortex, and it was long thought that the neocortex was the necessary base for advanced cognitive skills (Güntürkün & Bugnyar, 2016). However, we know today that some bird species, such as parrots and corvids like ravens and crows, have exceptional cognitive abilities comparable to those of great apes, despite having a brain without a cortex that that weigh only up to 25 grams (in comparison: the brain of a chimpanzee weights about 400 grams on average) (Güntürkün et al., 2024). Ravens can, for example, plan for future events, New Caledonian Crows can use tools to extract food, and sulfur-crested cockatoos can open household waste bins (Güntürkün et al., 2024). Thus, it is not the size of the brain that determines its abilities, but rather its contents. All these bird species have a brain area similar to the human prefrontal cortex, which is relevant for executive functions, and have other neuroanatomical features such as a large number of associative neurons with dense dopaminergic innervations, which allow them to show such amazing abilities. Thus, "bird brain" should not be an insult, but rather a compliment!

Pain in invertebrates: is it okay to boil a lobster alive?

Lobsters are a species of aquatic invertebrates that are eaten as seafood around the world. A traditional method of preparing them for consumption is to boil or steam them alive to ensure maximal freshness. The rationale behind this preparation method is that, for a long time, people thought that lobsters, unlike vertebrates commonly consumed as food (such as pigs or cows), have a more primitive nervous system and do not feel pain. Thus, while it would be unimaginable for most people to boil a pig or a calf alive, since these vertebrate animals clearly feel pain, some believe it is acceptable to do so with lobsters. However, recent research has revealed that the assumption that lobsters do not feel pain is likely wrong based on several criteria (Birch et al., 2021). There is strong evidence that lobsters have nociceptors, specialised nerve endings that perceive pain. Why would they have pain receptors if they do not feel pain? They also have integrative regions in their nervous system, which could integrate pain with other perceptions (such as being in a pot of boiling water). Painkillers have also been shown to affect the behaviour of lobsters, which would not be the case if they could not process pain. Thus, taken together, lobsters likely feel pain, and it is not okay to boil them alive. Based on this line of research, some governments, like those of Switzerland and New Zealand, have now made the practice of boiling lobsters alive illegal. This highlights the importance of research in informed decisions about animal welfare.

Conclusion

Psychobiology has yielded tremendous insights into how the human brain works, and it can also help us understand how animal brains work. Understanding whether animals show consciousness, emotions, pain, and other abilities that humans possess is crucial for animal welfare and how we as humans interact with pets and livestock.

Further reading

Additional academic source: Andrews, K. (2020). *The Animal Mind.* (2nd ed.). Routledge.

Additional academic source: De Waal, F. (2019). *Mama's Last Hug: Animal Emotions and What They Tell Us about Ourselves.* Norton.

Related documentary: *Inside the Mind of a Dog* (2024). A documentary about scientific insights into dog behaviour and thinking.

References

Birch, J., Burn, C., Schnell, A., Browning, H., & Crump, A. (2021). *Review of the Evidence of Sentience in Cephalopod Molluscs and Decapod Crustaceans.* LSE Consulting. LSE Enterprise Ltd. The London School of Economics and Political Science.

Birch, J., Schnell, A. K., & Clayton, N. S. (2020). Dimensions of animal consciousness. *Trends in Cognitive Sciences, 24*, 789–801. https://doi.org/10.1016/j.tics.2020.07.007

Güntürkün, O., & Bugnyar, T. (2016). Cognition without cortex. *Trends in Cognitive Sciences, 20*, 291–303. https://doi.org/10.1016/j.tics.2016.02.001

Güntürkün, O., Pusch, R., & Rose, J. (2024). Why birds are smart. *Trends in Cognitive Sciences, 28*, 197–209. https://doi.org/10.1016/j.tics.2023.11.002

Guran, C. A., Boch, M., Sladky, R., Lonardo, L., Karl, S., Huber, L., & Lamm, C. (2024). Functional mapping of the somatosensory cortex using noninvasive fMRI and touch in awake dogs. *Brain Structure and Function, 229*, 1193–1207. https://doi.org/10.1007/s00429-024-02798-0

Hillemacher, S., Ocklenburg, S., Güntürkün, O., & Tiemann, I. (2023). Roosters do not warn the bird in the mirror: the cognitive ecology of mirror self-recognition. *PLoS one, 18*, e0291416. https://doi.org/10.1371/journal.pone.0291416

Murray, L. E., Anderson, J. R., & Gallup, G. G., Jr. (2022). Mirror self-recognition in gorillas (Gorilla gorilla gorilla): a review and evaluation of mark test replications and variants. *Animal Cognition, 25*, 783–792. https://doi.org/10.1007/s10071-021-01592-3

Quaranta, A., Siniscalchi, M., & Vallortigara, G. (2007). Asymmetric tail-wagging responses by dogs to different emotive stimuli. *Current Biology, 17*, R199–R201. https://doi.org/10.1016/j.cub.2007.02.008

Chapter 17

The individual brain

Neurodiversity and the science of brain variability

Introduction

The human brain has evolved over millions of years, resulting in a shared structural and functional blueprint that is remarkably consistent across individuals. For example, each healthy brain has frontal, temporal, parietal, and occipital lobes and a cerebellum. Still, every brain is unique and works in different ways. The way we think, perceive the world, enjoy hobbies, solve puzzles, or experience emotions is influenced by different factors, including our genetics, the environment we grew up in, the way we were taught in school, and many more. Scientists are increasingly starting to recognise that brains vary on many different dimensions and how this variability can be important for understanding behaviour.

People vary in numerous ways: some are short while others are tall, we have different-shaped ears and noses, and all carry our own unique birthmarks. The brain is no exception. It can vary tremendously in anatomical characteristics such as size, weighing between 1.0 and 1.6 kg in adults, containing between 61 and 99 billion neurons, and having a **cortical surface area** (the total area of the folded cerebral cortex) spanning 1200 to 1800 cm^2, showing tremendous variation (Winkler et al., 2010). To make things more complicated, individual differences vary across different parts of the brain and also change with age, but not equally in all areas. For example, a study examining brain functional organisation found more functional variability amongst individuals in evolutionary-newer areas, like frontal and temporal association areas that integrate information from multiple sensory modalities, compared with areas that receive input from a single sensory modality (Mueller et al., 2013). These regions support functions such as language, social interaction,

Cortical surface area: The total area of the folded cerebral cortex.

DOI: 10.4324/9781003571537-21

and complex decision-making. It is logical that these systems show greater personal variation since they are more strongly influenced by each person's environment, life, and learning experiences (see Chapter 4).

Brain variability and variability in neurocognitive functioning

Can brain variations be linked to creativity? Or does social media scrolling reshape the brain networks responsible for focus? The quest to understand how variations within the brain relate to differences in behavioural performance is fundamental to psychobiology. Modern neuroimaging techniques (see Chapter 8) make it possible to ask whether almost any behaviour might be reflected in the brain, such as the amount of grey matter in certain regions or the size of a person's cortical surface. One study, for example, found that people who spent more time on a popular social media platform tended to have smaller grey matter volumes in the nucleus accumbens, a brain area central to reward and addiction (Montag et al., 2017). However, findings linking brain structure to behaviour are not always replicable. One reason may be that MRI studies often rely on small sample sizes due to their high cost. In fact, samples of around 1,000 participants have been suggested as necessary to reliably link brain regions to personality variables (Kharabian Masouleh et al., 2019). In addition, behaviour is increasingly understood to arise from distributed neural networks rather than single brain regions, meaning that multiple brain variables may need to be considered simultaneously.

The individual brain

As in many other disciplines, research in psychobiology has a long history of examining the "average" response. For example, imagine a theory that a particular brain structure, such as the hippocampus, is smaller in people with major depressive disorder, as these individuals often have memory issues and difficulty managing their emotions in a balanced way. The classic approach would be to invite a group of individuals with major depressive disorder to take part in MRI scanning, along with a group of individuals without the disorder, and compare the average size of the hippocampus in the two groups to see whether they differ. This average approach is useful for many research questions: it can help us identify biological systems that are more generally involved in a task or a condition, or when we want to evaluate general treatment effects related to things like antidepressants. In other words, the average approach is useful when the goal is to identify common patterns in individuals. However, what makes this approach useful can also be limiting, as we sometimes want to examine variability within groups rather than between groups.

> **Lateralised:** The concept that some brain functions are specialised to one side of the brain.

Let us consider handedness as an example. Left-handers, who constitute approximately 10% of the population, are often excluded from psychobiological studies because early research indicated that their brains are organised differently from right-handers as groups, not because they perform better or worse on tasks. This led to the perception that left-handers are simply "different". However, adopting an individual differences perspective reveals that there is no distinct "right-handed" or "left-handed" brain. Instead, left-handers show greater variability in how they process information, such as language. You may have heard the common misconception that left-handers process language with their right hemisphere instead of the left. This is not true, but we do know that about 15% of left-handers process language more with the right side of their brain, and 15% use each side approximately equally. This highlights that brain functions can vary significantly, sometimes even being "flipped" from the typical pattern. One study set out to examine whether individuals with a reversed brain organisation also show reversed patterns of other lateralised functions (the concept that some brain functions are specialised to one side of the brain) (Karlsson et al., 2022). They recruited 27 people with right-sided language and scanned their brains when they performed two other lateralised tasks: a face and a body task. But the study did not find that all individuals had a reversal for processing faces or bodies. In fact, the distribution was about 50/50, and some people had faces reversed but not bodies, and vice versa, making their cognitive patterns more unique. Recognising not only differences between groups but also differences between individuals in those groups is a valuable means of investigating the diverse ways in which the same cognitive information can be processed in the brain.

Differences in brain structure and function between people are also essential to the field of clinical psychobiology, which has long sought neural markers of psychiatric and neurodevelopmental disorders to understand underlying brain mechanisms and improve diagnostic accuracy. These studies have given us a wealth of important information, and research has found consistent patterns in the brain associated with many different mental health conditions. For example, the amygdala shows heightened responses to threat in anxiety and post-traumatic stress disorder (e.g., Hayes et al., 2012), while the hippocampus, which is critical for memory and emotion, is often reduced in volume in major depressive

Neurodivergent people: Those whose neurocognitive functioning diverges significantly from what is considered societal standards of "common" functioning.

Neurotypical people: Those whose cognitive functioning falls within defined norms.

disorders (Schmaal et al., 2016). While these findings have advanced our understanding of the biological basis of behaviour, they also often note substantial individual differences, which can make it difficult if you want to link certain brain aspects with behaviour.

Neurodiversity

What comes to mind when you hear "neurodiversity"? While it might sound like a term from psychobiological research on brain variability, it actually originated outside the lab. **Neurodiversity** broadly refers to the observation of the variation across humanity of neurocognitive functioning and traits and includes everyone, both **neurodivergent people**, those whose neurocognitive functioning diverges significantly from what is considered societal standards of "common" functioning, and **neurotypical people**, those whose cognitive functioning falls within defined norms. The term neurodiversity originated in the mid-1990s through discussions within the autism community. Since then, the concept of neurodiversity has come to encompass not only autism spectrum disorder but also other neurocognitive differences such as attention deficit hyperactivity disorder, dyslexia, learning disabilities, and more (Miranda--Ojeda et al., 2025). The neurodiversity paradigm highlights the inherent value in this variation, pointing out that ideas about what is "normal" or "right" are shaped by society and culture and can create power imbalances and lead to discrimination. Neurodiversity as a movement is a social and political effort that promotes the rights, recognition, and inclusion of neurodivergent individuals in various contexts (Zaneva et al., 2024).

Towards more inclusive psychobiological research

It is important for psychobiologists to consider neurodiversity in the way research is designed and interpreted. Psychobiological experiments are often developed by neurotypical researchers for neurotypical participants, which can disadvantage individuals who think or solve problems differently. For example, a long-standing conception in autism research has been that many individuals with autism lack a **theory of mind (ToM)**, the ability to understand that other people have thoughts, intentions, and perspectives different from one's own. Gernsbacher and Yergeau (2019) reviewed already published ToM experiments in individuals with autism and concluded that this idea is not supported by the available research. Instead, they showed that differences in task performance may simply reflect different reasoning strategies that are not accommodated in the tasks used. It reminds us that research can only be accurate and fair if it is inclusive, as it could otherwise reinforce harmful stereotypes. Including neurodiverse voices as collaborators or co-researchers is one way research can better reflect their experiences and perspectives. Diversity in thinking drives innovation and fuels better science.

Conclusion

There is no single way for the brain to function, and the variability we see across brains gives rise to our many personalities, characteristics, and quirks. We are learning more about how variability in human brain function and structure relates to behaviour. By examining individual differences, research can better understand the diverse ways in which people think, learn, and experience the world.

Further reading

Related book: Thomson, H. (2018). *Unthinkable: An Extraordinary Journey through the World's Strangest Brains.* Hachette. Popular science book on nine rare neurodisorders.

Related web resource: *Neurodivergence: Change, complexity, and challenge.* Special Issue of the Psychologist, a magazine by the BPS: https://www.bps.org.uk/psychologist-issue/2024/january/psychologist-januaryfebruary-2024

References

Gernsbacher, M. A., & Yergeau, M. (2019). Empirical failures of the claim that autistic people lack a theory of mind. *Archives of Scientific Psychology*, *7*(1), 102. https://doi.org/10.1037/arc0000067

Hayes, J. P., Hayes, S. M., & Mikedis, A. M. (2012). Quantitative meta-analysis of neural activity in posttraumatic stress disorder. *Biology of Mood & Anxiety Disorders*, *2*(1), 9. https://doi.org/10.1186/2045-5380-2-9

Karlsson, E. M., Johnstone, L. T., & Carey, D. P. (2022). Reciprocal or independent hemispheric specializations: evidence from cerebral dominance for fluency, faces, and bodies in right-and left-handers. *Psychology & Neuroscience*, *15*(2), 89. https://doi.org/10.1037/pne0000269

Kharabian Masouleh, S., Eickhoff, S. B., Hoffstaedter, F., Genon, S., & Alzheimer's Disease Neuroimaging Initiative. (2019). Empirical examination of the replicability of associations between brain structure and psychological variables. *eLife*, *8*, e43464. https://doi.org/10.7554/eLife.43464

Miranda-Ojeda, R., Wickramasinghe, A., Ntolkeras, G., Castanho, I., & Yassin, W. (2025). The neurodiversity framework in medicine: on the Spectrum. *Developmental Neurobiology*, *85*(1), e22960. https://doi.org/10.1002/dneu.22960

Montag, C., Markowetz, A., Blaszkiewicz, K., Andone, I., Lachmann, B., Sariyska, R., Trendafilov, B., Eibes, M., Kolb, J., Reuter, M., Weber, B., & Markett, S. (2017). Facebook usage on smartphones and gray matter volume of the nucleus accumbens. *Behavioural Brain Research*, *329*, 221–228. https://doi.org/10.1016/j.bbr.2017.04.035

Mueller, S., Wang, D., Fox, M. D., Yeo, B. T., Sepulcre, J., Sabuncu, M. R., Shafee, R., Lu, J., & Liu, H. (2013). Individual variability in functional connectivity architecture of the human brain. *Neuron*, *77*(3), 586–595. https://doi.org/10.1016/j.neuron.2012.12.028

Schmaal, L., Veltman, D. J., van Erp, T. G., Sämann, P. G., Frodl, T., Jahanshad, N., Loehrer, E., Tiemeier, H., Hofman, A., Niessen, W. J., Vernooij, M. W., Ikram, M. A., Wittfeld, K., Grabe, H. J., Block, A., Hegenscheid, K., Völzke, H., Hoehn, D., Czisch, M., ... Hibar, D. P. (2016). Subcortical brain alterations in major depressive disorder: findings from the ENIGMA Major Depressive Disorder working group. *Molecular Psychiatry*, *21*(6), 806–812. https://doi.org/10.1038/mp.2015.69

Winkler, A. M., Kochunov, P., Blangero, J., Almasy, L., Zilles, K., Fox, P. T., Duggirala, R., & Glahn, D. C. (2010). Cortical thickness or grey matter volume? The importance of selecting the phenotype for imaging genetics studies. *Neuroimage*, *53*(3), 1135–1146. https://doi.org/10.1016/j.neuroimage.2009.12.028

Zaneva, M., Coll-Martín, T., Héjja-Brichard, Y., Kalandadze, T., Kis, A., Koperska, A., Manalili, M. A. R., Mathy, A., Graham, C. J., Hollis, A., Ross, R. M., Yeung, S. K., Allen, V., Azevedo, F., Friedel, E., Fuller, S., Giannouli, V., Gjoneska, B., Hartmann, H., ... Zisk, A. H. (2024). An annotated introductory reading list for neurodiversity. *Elife*, *13*, e102467. https://doi.org/10.7554/eLife.102467

Chapter 18

I'm so stressed

Physical health, mental health, immune system, and the neurobiology of stress

Introduction

After weeks of relentless deadlines, late-night revision sessions coupled with copious amounts of tea and energy drinks, and the kind of stress that makes your brain feel like you are constantly walking around on a bed of clouds in an alternative reality, Eddie finally handed in his last assignment of the year and felt an unfamiliar wave of relief. It was December, and the holiday season was upon him. It was finally time for cosy markets and mulled wine! Of course, his body had other plans. The sore throat arrived first, followed by a pounding headache and complete shutdown, as if his immune system had been running on borrowed time and instant noodles from the local grocery store. The moment the pressure lifted, his body crumbled, reminding him that rest is not an optional part of life.

Stress is often described as a condition in which external or internal pressures outweigh the body's ability to cope, therefore triggering a stress response to manage the challenge. In daily life, we encounter many different stressors. These include societal stressors, such as the COVID-19 pandemic, economic uncertainty, and climate change. We also experience a range of personal and work-related stressors. In the UK, a national survey found that 83% among 18–24-year-olds had felt so stressed at some point in the previous year that they felt overwhelmed or unable to cope (Mental Health Foundation, 2018). Stress is also recognised as a major contributor to long-term sickness absence. In 2024, 964,000 workers in the UK reported work-related stress, depression, or anxiety, resulting in 22.1 million lost working days (Health and Safety Executive, 2025a, 2025b). Stress is also a major factor in mental health, as it increases the risk of anxiety and depression. As such, stress places a significant burden on individuals, workplaces, and society as a whole. As we will see in the next sections, psychobiological research has made many important contributions to understanding the stress response.

DOI: 10.4324/9781003571537-22

The stress response

Stress is a part of everyday life, and something that everyone experiences at least occasionally. You have probably heard the expression "a little stress is good for you", and this is not necessarily untrue. The human body adapts to its environment, and the stress response is part of this adaptation. Imagine that you are about to enter an important exam. The mild stress experienced in that moment can help you focus. If you have an important sports game to play, stress can help improve reactions and endurance during the game. As stress can be caused by so many different factors, it is no surprise that it also involves a lot of different psychobiological processes in the CNS and beyond.

Two main systems activate when we experience stress: the **sympathetic–adrenal–medullary (SAM) system** and the **hypothalamic–pituitary–adrenal (HPA) axis** (O'Connor et al., 2021). The SAM system is easiest to activate. When a person perceives a threat, the brain, first the amygdala, then the hypothalamus, quickly activates the autonomic nervous system (ANS). The ANS sends a signal to the adrenal glands, instructing them to release the hormones epinephrine (also known as adrenaline) and norepinephrine (or noradrenaline). These hormones influence several bodily systems: breathing speeds up, the heart beats faster and stronger, the pupils widen to let in more light, and digestion slows down so more blood can be sent to the muscles. This is the SAM system initiating the body's rapid response to stress. Within seconds, both adrenaline and noradrenaline prepare the entire body for immediate action, also known as the fight-or-flight response.

Besides the fast-acting fight-or-flight response, the body also has a slower stress system. The hypothalamus releases a hormone called corticotropin-releasing hormone that travels to the pituitary gland, which then releases another hormone called adrenocorticotropic hormone (ACTH). ACTH moves through the bloodstream to the **adrenal cortex**, the outer part of the adrenal gland, causing it to produce adrenal **steroids** (organic compounds with a specific molecular structure) like cortisol, also called the stress hormone.

Sympathetic–adrenal–medullary (SAM) system: System that regulates the body's fast "fight-or-flight" stress response.

Hypothalamic–pituitary–adrenal (HPA) axis: System that regulates the body's hormonal stress response.

Adrenal cortex: The outer layer of the adrenal glands, two small glands that produce hormones.

> **Steroids:** Organic compounds with a specific molecular structure.
>
> **Acute stress**: The body's short-term response to immediate physical or mental stressors.
>
> **Chronic stress:** Long-term stressor over weeks, months, or years.

The HPA regulates both the production of cortisol and the amount that is released into the bloodstream. During stress, cortisol helps the body access extra energy by releasing stored fuels from the muscles and liver and converting them into glucose for the brain and body to use. Cortisol also increases heart rate, blood pressure, and breathing frequency, thus preparing the body for a fight-or-flight reaction to a threat. In addition, cortisol can enhance alertness and decision-making, while also influencing the immune response, preparing the body for potential danger (see below). Once the stressor has passed, the body gradually deactivates its stress-response systems and goes back to its original state.

When is stress bad?

Stress exists on a spectrum from **acute stress** that only lasts for short periods, like exam stress, to stress that is experienced over weeks, months, or years: **chronic stress**. This type of stress can, for example, be experienced with relationship problems, financial hardships, or social isolation and loneliness.

As previously mentioned, the stress response is part of how the body adapts to challenges. Once the stressful situation ends, the body is supposed to switch off this response and return to its usual balance. However, if the stress response stays active for too long, the body remains in a state of high alert. Over time, the brain will adjust to this constant activation, a process called allostasis. According to the allostatic load model proposed by McEwen (1998), chronic stress leads to wear and tear on the body, which is detrimental to health, putting strain on almost every part of the body. For example, chronic stress will result in increased or decreased levels of cortisol in the body. Long-term stress can also change how genes work in the brain, both directly through the influence of stress hormones but also indirectly through modifications of DNA and proteins that influence gene activity. High levels of cortisone can damage neurons in the hippocampus, the part of the brain important for memory and learning, or in the prefrontal cortex, which is important for emotion and decision-making. These changes make it harder for the brain to regulate several behaviours beyond stress, such as thinking, emotions, and memory. Chronic stress can also impact health indirectly, by influencing health

Post-traumatic stress disorder (PTSD): A mental health condition that can develop following traumatic stress.

Hyperarousal: The feeling of being constantly on edge or easily startled.

Immune system: The body's defence from pathogens such as viruses and bacteria.

behaviours such as sleep, diet, and exercise. These combined effects increase allostatic load and raise the risk for mental and physical health problems.

Stress and mental health

Sustained, chronic, and traumatic stress has severe negative consequences and can harm mental health. Stress is a key element in developing mental health problems such as depression and anxiety. In depression, the HPA axis often functions abnormally, and cortisol levels stay high for prolonged periods. This can lead to symptoms like feeling hopeless, having trouble sleeping, and changes in appetite. **Post-traumatic stress disorder (PTSD)** is a mental health condition that can develop following traumatic stress (Ressler et al., 2022). Traumatic stress refers to stress that is experienced due to extremely stressful or terrifying events, such as witnessing or experiencing a serious injury. People with PTSD often relive the trauma through intrusive memories, flashbacks, or nightmares, and many consequently avoid any reminders of the event. They often experience ongoing negative emotions such as guilt and fear and have difficulties with memory and concentration. They often experience **hyperarousal**, meaning they may feel constantly on edge or easily startled. PTSD is linked with abnormal fear responses. Activation in the amygdala, which processes threat and fear, is increased, while activation in the prefrontal cortex and hippocampus is decreased. As a result, the brain's threat-response system remains active even in safe situations. The amygdala also influences other systems in the brain, including the HPA axis. Dysregulation of these systems contributes to many of the psychological and physiological symptoms observed in PTSD.

Psychological stress and the immune system

Why do we so often get sick after long, stressful situations as soon as we try to relax? Although brief stress may improve the function of the **immune system**, our body's defence from pathogens such as viruses and bacteria, long-lasting stress has the opposite effect. The immune system is critical for human health and interacts closely with our hormonal and nervous systems. Acute stress causes immune cells to move from storage into the blood and then to organs (where injury is most likely), boosting the body's defences. This is because, evolutionarily, stress was a reliable signal of impending physical danger resulting in wounds or infection, and therefore, why our immune system is boosted during adaptive stressful situations.

> **Cytokines:** Small signalling proteins released by immune cells during inflammation.

Long-term stress impacts not only emotions and behaviours, such as coping skills and sleep, but also affects the body's physiological functions, including the immune system. This makes it easier to catch colds or for wounds to take longer to heal. As mentioned earlier, cortisol also plays an important role in immune health. The HPA axis helps regulate immune response through negative feedback, reducing its activity when it is no longer needed. However, if stress hormones such as cortisol malfunction, the inflammation response in the body can increase instead of decrease. This can happen in two ways: either the body produces less cortisol, losing its natural anti-inflammatory effect, or it produces too much, causing receptors to become resistant and less responsive. In both cases, decreased anti-inflammatory feedback leads to increased inflammation. Over time, this extra inflammation makes the immune system work less efficiently, so the body has a harder time fighting off germs and therefore staying healthy. Inflammation in the body also plays a major role in conditions like major depressive disorder (Feng et al., 2025). **Cytokines** are small signalling proteins released by immune cells during inflammation. Some of these can already enter the brain, but most are kept out by the blood–brain barrier. However, chronic inflammation in the body can make the blood–brain barrier less effective, letting more cytokines into the brain. In the brain, cytokines can disrupt neurotransmission of, for example, serotonin, which, amongst other things, can lead to depressive symptoms.

Why does stress impact people so differently?

Have you ever noticed that some people thrive in situations you would pay good money to avoid? Skydiving, for example, is seen as highly thrilling by some but anxiety provoking for others. Scientists have identified a range of factors that influence how people react to stress. Genetic factors (see Chapter 9), for example, can play a large role. Genetics is thought to play a 30–40% role in who will develop PTSD and who will not (Ressler et al., 2022). In addition, a large GWAS on depression identified the HPA axis as one of the key gene pathways linked with depression risk (Wray et al., 2018). This means that susceptibility to depression is closely tied to how a person reacts to stress. Stress responses are also influenced by multiple factors. Brain regions such as the amygdala, prefrontal cortex, and hippocampus all affect how we perceive and manage threats. Cognitive factors, such as coping styles, resilience, and personality, also play a role. A person's history of trauma is another key factor, as individuals who experienced significant stress or trauma in childhood are often more vulnerable to stress later in life. Finally, the social environment strongly influences coping: having stable relationships and reliable social support can help people manage stress more effectively. Together, these biological, cognitive, experiential, and social factors interact to determine how stress is experienced and managed.

Managing stress

I hope you, after reading this chapter, understand how important managing stress is in life. It is not just about mental wellness, it is a real biological intervention, calming the body's stress response and increasing overall health. Recently, there has been a new trend of so-called "rage rooms" popping up across the country – where the idea is that you relieve stress and anger by breaking things. However, recently scientists looked at the effectiveness of these interventions and found that fighting stress and anger with anger does not actually work that well (Kjærvik & Bushman, 2024). Mind-body practices such as mindfulness, yoga, or breathing exercises do help, as do good sleep and social connection. So, if you need an excuse to cook a healthy meal, laugh with friends, or just spend time with loved ones, here it is.

Conclusion

Stress is a part of the body's natural response to the environment. However, prolonged periods of stress alter normal brain functioning in many different ways and can have severe consequences for both physical and mental health.

Further reading

Additional academic source: Reed, R. G., Raison, C. L. (2016). Stress and the immune system. In: Esser, C. (Ed.). *Environmental Influences on the Immune System*. Springer. https://doi.org/10.1007/978-3-7091-1890-0_5

Related documentary: Mindfulness (Season 1, Episode 4), in The Mind, Explained. (2019, September 12). Netflix.

Relevant web resource: https://www.mentalhealth.org.uk/explore-mental-health/a-z-topics/stress A website from the Mental Health Foundation with information about and how to combat stress

Relevant web resource: https://www.mind.org.uk/information-support/types-of-mental-health-problems/stress/ A website from the organisation Mind with information about and how to combat stress

Relevant web resource: https://www.bps.org.uk/topics?term=Stress%20and%20anxiety, a web resource on stress and anxiety from the BPS.

References

Feng, X., Jia, M., Cai, M., Zhu, T., Hashimoto, K., & Yang, J. J. (2025). Central-peripheral neuroimmune dynamics in psychological stress and depression: insights from current research. *Molecular Psychiatry*, *30*(10), 4881–4898. https://doi.org/10.1038/s41380-025-03085-y

Health and Safety Executive. (2025a). *Work-Related Stress, Anxiety or Depression Statistics in Great Britain, 2024*. HSE. https://www.hse.gov.uk/statistics/overview.htm

Health and Safety Executive. (2025b). *Working Days Lost: Stress, Depression or Anxiety*. HSE. https://www.hse.gov.uk/statistics/dayslost.htm

Kjærvik, S. L., & Bushman, B. J. (2024). A meta-analytic review of anger management activities that increase or decrease arousal: what fuels or douses rage? *Clinical Psychology Review*, *109*, 102414. https://doi.org/10.1016/j.cpr.2024.102414

McEwen, B. S. (1998). Stress, adaptation, and disease: allostasis and allostatic load. *Annals of the New York Academy of Sciences*, *840*(1), 33–44. https://doi.org/10.1111/j.1749-6632.1998.tb09546.x

Mental Health Foundation. (2018, May). *Stress: Are We Coping?* Mental Health Foundation. https://www.mentalhealth.org.uk/sites/default/files/2022-08/stress-are-we-coping.pdf

O'Connor, D. B., Thayer, J. F., & Vedhara, K. (2021). Stress and health: a review of psychobiological processes. *Annual Review of Psychology*, *72*(1), 663–688. https://doi.org/10.1146/annurev-psych-062520-122331

Ressler, K. J., Berretta, S., Bolshakov, V. Y., Rosso, I. M., Meloni, E. G., Rauch, S. L., & Carlezon, W. A., Jr. (2022). Post-traumatic stress disorder: clinical and translational neuroscience from cells to circuits. *Nature Reviews Neurology*, *18*(5), 273–288. https://doi.org/10.1038/s41582-022-00635-8

Wray, N. R., Ripke, S., Mattheisen, M., Trzaskowski, M., Byrne, E. M., Abdellaoui, A., Adams, M. J., Agerbo, E., Air, T. M., Andlauer, T. M. F., Bacanu, S.-A., Bækvad-Hansen, M., Beekman, A. F. T., Bigdeli, T. B., Binder, E. B., Blackwood, D. R. H., Bryois, J., Buttenschøn, H. N., Bybjerg-Grauholm, J., … Sullivan, P. F. (2018). Genome-wide association analyses identify 44 risk variants and refine the genetic architecture of major depression. *Nature Genetics*, *50*(5), 668–681. https://doi.org/10.1038/s41588-018-0090-3

Section 5

Key emerging areas

This concluding section provides an overview of topics likely to receive increased attention in psychobiological research in the coming years and decades. These include climate psychobiology and the psychobiology of human and artificial intelligence.

At the end of section five, you will:

- Know how the climate affects brain function
- Have learned about human intelligence
- Have gained knowledge about the role of artificial intelligence as a tool to analyse psychobiological data
- Have gained insights about whether using artificial intelligence too much in daily life may negatively affect human intelligence

DOI: 10.4324/9781003571537-23

Chapter 19

Climate psychobiology and the future of the planet

Introduction

In the chapters on neuroplasticity and genetics, we already discussed the tremendous importance of environmental influences on the human brain. Climate psychobiology, one of the key emerging areas in psychobiology, is also concerned with how the environment affects the brain, behaviour, and mental health. In 2022, Antonio Guterres, the Secretary-General of the United Nations, famously stated that humanity is on its way to climate hell, with one foot still on the accelerator (United Nations, 2022). The climate crisis is one of the greatest threats to human physical and mental health, according to the World Health Organization. It is estimated that between 2030 and 2050, the climate crisis will cause a quarter of a million deaths per year from causes such as heat stress and malnutrition (World Health Organization, 2023). From a psychological perspective, extreme weather events such as tropical storms or wildfires clearly contribute to mental health issues like post-traumatic stress disorder (PTSD) or depression. While much of the psychological research on the climate crisis focuses on mental health, studies on psychobiology are also increasing (Metzen & Ocklenburg, 2024). The climate crisis affects brain structure and function on multiple levels. The first of these levels is direct exposure to an extreme weather event such as a flood, a forest fire, or a major storm. Less severe changes in environmental conditions can also have significant impacts. These, for example, include stress caused by heat waves as well as effects from air or water pollution. Even those not directly affected by adverse climate changes may experience its psychological impact, as media coverage of the climate crisis can elicit so-called "climate emotions" such as climate anxiety, climate depression, and climate anger. Although climate and geopolitical anxiety are not currently diagnosable conditions in the most recent version of the Diagnostic and Statistical Manual of Mental Disorders (DSM-5), they are still recognised by mental health professionals and psychologists as legitimate, rational, and growing responses to world instability and the climate crisis. Below,

DOI: 10.4324/9781003571537-24

we highlight recent psychobiological research on how nature, in general, and the effects of the climate crisis, specifically, affect brain structure and function.

Environmental neuroscience

Climate psychobiology can be understood as a subfield of **environmental neuroscience**, an emerging field of neuroscience that focuses on how the physical environment influences the brain and vice versa (Kühn, 2024). For example, environmental neuroscientists have investigated how urban versus rural upbringings affect mental health, as well as brain structure and function. They have also explored the positive effects of spending time in nature on brain functions related to stress. For example, a recent functional magnetic resonance imaging (fMRI) study tested participants inside an magnetic resonance imaging (MRI) scanner using a fearful faces task, which typically activates the amygdala, an important brain centre for processing negative emotions, as well as a stress-inducing task (Sudimac et al., 2022). The researchers then divided the participants into two groups: one took a 60-minute walk in a natural forest and the other took a 60-minute walk in an urban environment. Before the walk, both groups showed similar amygdala activation in response to fearful faces. However, after the walk, the forest group showed significantly reduced amygdala activation compared to the urban group. This shows how spending time in an undamaged natural environment can down-regulate activity in brain regions related to stress and negative emotions and highlights the importance of intact natural environments for mental health. Whether environments destroyed as a consequence of the climate crisis (e.g., burned-down forests, flooded areas, and areas destroyed by hurricanes) also increase stress is an important emerging question in psychobiology that future studies will need to investigate.

> **Environmental neuroscience**: An emerging field of neuroscience that focuses on how the physical environment influences the brain and vice versa.

Extreme weather events, trauma, and the brain

In January 2025, a series of wildfires killed more than 20 people and destroyed thousands of homes in Southern California. Witnessing one's belongings go up in flames and fighting for survival can be highly traumatising, and studies show that up to 40% of people exposed to such extreme weather events later face psychological problems (Clayton et al., 2017). PTSD is the most common psychological disorder following such events. On average, 15–20% of those directly exposed to wildfires, floods, or hurricanes subsequently develop PTSD.

Studies on brain changes in PTSD show that the condition can lead to a dysregulation of the hypothalamic–pituitary–adrenal axis, a major stress-processing pathway (see Chapter 18 on stress for details). While acute stress leads to higher levels of the stress hormone cortisol, PTSD leads to chronically lower cortisol levels, which results in a distorted processing of stressful incidents. PTSD also leads to increased amygdala activity, a brain area central to the processing of negative emotions, as well as reduced activity in the hippocampus, a brain area central to memory. Although these studies have largely been performed with veterans, victims of violence, and other groups with PTSD, it is an important future direction for psychobiological research to also conduct these studies in patients with PTSD due to the effects of the climate crisis.

The psychobiology of heat

Have you ever noticed how the outside temperature affects your mood, ability to think, or other psychological processes? Have you, for example, ever found it hard to study or work during a particularly hot week in summer? If so, you are not alone. Many people report difficulty concentrating during heat waves, and there is a psychobiological explanation for this phenomenon. Healthy people have an average body temperature of about 37°C. The temperature of the brain is slightly above that, with an average of 38.5°C. Some brain areas reach an average temperature of 40°C, which is equivalent to a mild fever in the body. However, this does not mean that the brain functions best at such high external temperatures. Research suggests that the optimal outside temperature to perform taxing cognitive tasks, like studying for an exam in psychobiology or filing a tax report, ranges from approximately 23 to 27°C. Anything hotter than that and our cognitive abilities begin to suffer. The reason for this may be that heat differentially affects brain network functions. Specifically, it has been shown to impair the executive control network, which is relevant for higher cognitive functions. In contrast, the orienting and alerting networks relevant for more basic processes, like where to put attention were not affected (Löhmus, 2018). Other experiments have also shown that volunteers are worse at solving cognitively demanding tasks in high heat. In addition to affecting neural networks and impairing cognitive functions, high heat also negatively impacts sleep. Many people have issues falling asleep when the room is too hot, such as on a particularly warm summer night. Many mental health disorders are accompanied by sleeping disturbances, and struggling to fall or stay asleep for several nights can lead to a negative mood, as well as problems with attention, learning, and memory (Löhmus, 2018). Therefore, sleeping disturbances caused by heat waves can both exacerbate mental health issues and impair cognitive abilities in affected people.

The psychobiology of air pollution

Clean air is essential for both mental and physical well-being, and pollution from wildfires can have serious adverse health effects. In the summer of 2022, news headlines reported that the rock band Pearl Jam had to cancel a concert in Vienna after singer Eddie Vedder's throat was damaged by smoke from wildfires raging in France at the time. The negative effects of wildfire smoke made the news even more prominently in June 2023. Storms over Nova Scotia pushed smoke from several wildfires in Canada into New York, turning the sky into a gloomy post-apocalyptic orange. Doctors reported an increase in patients complaining about burning eyes, breathing difficulties, and other health issues. In addition to these physical symptoms, a **systematic review** of psychobiological and mental health studies on air pollution revealed several different key insights (Xie et al., 2023). The review showed clear evidence that air pollution increases the risk of depression. On the psychobiological side, several studies reported a decreased volume of grey matter in neural circuits involving the cortex, striatum, and thalamus, brain areas relevant for executive function, emotion, and reward processing. Most prominently, air pollution affects neural circuits relevant to emotional regulation, attention, and impulsive behaviour. Moreover, studies have also reported that children growing up in cities with high air pollution show lesions in the white matter underlying the prefrontal cortex, a central area for decision-making and executive functions, and the corpus callosum, the connection between the two halves of the brain. The lesions in important white matter networks connecting brain areas relevant for higher-order cognition may adversely affect their cognitive abilities in the long run.

> **Systematic review**: A type of scientific article that contains a synthesis of empirical research findings on a topic that has been performed using defined systematic guidelines on how to perform a literature search and literature extraction.

How could inhaling wildfire smoke have such negative effects on the brain? Xie et al. (2023) suggested a model in which air pollutants lead to peripheral inflammation in the lung. This prompts the release of several cytokines, a type of cell signalling molecule, which is especially important in the immune system (see Chapter 18). Both air pollutants and cytokines enter the bloodstream. While air pollutants can damage cells, some cytokines, unfortunately, increase the permeability of the blood–brain barrier. This has the effect that molecules from the peripheral bloodstream that would normally not be able to reach the brain due to the blood-brain barrier may now reach the brain and potentially cause harmful effects there. Moreover, when microglia destroy the air pollutants in the bloodstream, they also release molecules that cause inflammation. Together, these effects can lead to damage in the brain if the air pollution is long-lasting or particularly severe.

Towards a more climate-friendly psychobiology

As socially and environmentally conscious researchers, it is important to consider and reflect critically on the environmental impact of our research practices (Rae et al., 2022). Conducting an fMRI study, for example, can have a large **carbon footprint** due to its energy-intensive nature. The carbon footprint is a value that indicates how much carbon dioxide (CO_2) is produced by an activity or process (such as scanning a participant in an MRI scanner). Determining the carbon footprint of different psychobiological methods allows us to identify the most environmentally sustainable choice. In the case of fMRI, not only does using and maintaining the MRI scanner have a high carbon footprint since operating the scanner needs a lot of energy, but it is also energy intensive to store the data and perform different analyses. An important solution to reduce the carbon footprint of psychobiological research is the greater sharing and reuse of existing datasets. As part of the open science movement, many openly available psychobiological datasets are accessible on platforms like the Open Science Framework. By reusing existing data when possible instead of collecting new data, the carbon footprint of fMRI research can be reduced significantly. Other aspects of psychobiological research that can be made more climate-friendly include reducing

> **Carbon footprint**: A value that indicates how much carbon dioxide (CO_2) is caused by an activity or process (such as scanning a participant in an MRI scanner). Determining the carbon footprint of different psychobiological methods allows us to identify the most environmentally sustainable choice.

flights to conferences by using more sustainable modes of transportation and establishing sustainability committees within research institutions (Rae et al., 2022). As active scientists in psychobiology, we must take our responsibility towards society and the planet seriously, aiming to make our research on the climate crisis as climate-friendly as possible!

Conclusion

Understanding how the climate crisis affects the body and the brain is one of the most important key emerging areas in psychobiology. However, psychobiological research on both direct and indirect effects of the climate crisis on brain structure and function is still in its infancy. It will no doubt be a major research topic for decades to come. Both controlled experiments and longitudinal neuroimaging and biomarker studies assessing how the direct and indirect effects of the climate crisis affect the brain are critically important to gain a mechanistic understanding of the underlying processes. In addition, psychobiology can not only help in understanding the effects of the climate crisis but also by providing information on how prevention measures can be designed efficiently. For example, the psychobiology of decision-making can be highly relevant to understanding how climate-relevant consumer, policy, or investment strategies are made. Moreover, psychobiological research on motivation can help in understanding what motivates people to change their behaviour towards a more environmentally friendly lifestyle (e.g., not eating meat, not booking cruises, and so on).

Further reading

Additional academic source: Metzen, D., & Ocklenburg, S. (2024). *The Psychology and Neuroscience of the Climate Crisis. How Our Brain Reacts to Climate Change*. Springer.

Related documentary: *Climate Change - The Facts* (2019). A documentary narrated by Sir David Attenborough focused on the science explaining the climate crisis.

Relevant web resource: The climate and ecological crisis position statement by the BPS is highlights the role that psychologists play in understanding and fighting the climate crisis: https://cms.bps.org.uk/sites/default/files/2023-10/BPS%20Position%20Statement%20on%20the%20Climate%20and%20Ecological%20Crisis.pdf

References

Clayton, S., Manning, C. M., Krygsman, K., & Speiser, M. (2017). *Mental Health and Our Changing Climate: Impacts, Implications, and Guidance*. American Psychological Association, and ecoAmerica.

Kühn, S. (Ed.). (2024). *Environmental Neuroscience*. Springer.

Löhmus, M. (2018). Possible biological mechanisms linking mental health and heat-a contemplative review. *International Journal of Environmental Research and Public Health, 15*, 1515. https://doi.org/10.3390/ijerph15071515

Rae, C. L., Farley, M., Jeffery, K. J., & Urai, A. E. (2022). Climate crisis and ecological emergency: why they concern (neuro)scientists, and what we can do. *Brain and Neuroscience Advances, 6*, 23982128221075430. https://doi.org/10.1177/23982128221075430

Sudimac, S., Sale, V., & Kühn, S. (2022). How nature nurtures: amygdala activity decreases as the result of a one-hour walk in nature. *Molecular Psychiatry, 27*, 4446–4452. https://doi.org/10.1038/s41380-022-01720-6

United Nations. (2022). *Secretary-General's remarks to High-Level opening of COP27*. Retrieved 19 February 2025 from https://www.un.org/sg/en/content/sg/speeches/2022-11-07/secretary-generals-remarks-high-level-opening-of-cop27

Xie, H., Cao, Y., Li, J., Lyu, Y., Roberts, N., & Jia, Z. (2023). Affective disorder and brain alterations in children and adolescents exposed to outdoor air pollution. *Journal of Affective Disorders, 331*, 413–424. https://doi.org/10.1016/j.jad.2023.03.082

World Health Organization. (2023). *Climate Change*. Retrieved 23 February 2025 from https://www.who.int/news-room/fact-sheets/detail/climate-change-and-health

Chapter 20

The psychobiology of intelligence and the age of artificial intelligence

Introduction

One of the key emerging areas in psychobiological research (and psychological research in general) is how **artificial intelligence (AI)** will affect the way we conduct psychobiological research and, in turn, whether these insights about human intelligence can be useful in designing better AI systems. In general, **human intelligence** refers to the ability of the human brain to perform complex cognitive tasks. These may include activities such as writing an essay on neurodiversity for a psychology class, completing a 1000-piece puzzle, or mentally rotating complex three-dimensional objects. Intelligence consists of several different subcomponents. Early theories divided intelligence into fluid intelligence, the ability to solve new cognitive challenges quickly and accurately, and crystallised intelligence, the knowledge about the world a person acquired over their lifetime. Another idea proposes that intelligence is made from different subcomponents based on cognitive domains, such as verbal intelligence, non-verbal intelligence, spatial intelligence, emotional intelligence, social intelligence, and many more. Human intelligence is often measured with tests that yield an intelligence quotient, which reflects ability across different domains. AI refers to the ability of computer software to perform complex cognitive tasks similar to or better than those of the human brain. This can refer to verbal intelligence (such as in AI models that generate text), but also spatial intelligence (as in AI models that perform complex scientific tasks that require spatial modulation, such as simulation of protein folding).

> **Artificial intelligence (AI):** The ability of software to perform complex cognitive tasks.
>
> **Human intelligence**: The ability of the human brain to perform complex cognitive tasks.

DOI: 10.4324/9781003571537-25

What do we know about the psychobiology of human intelligence and can it help us build better artificial intelligence software?

The human brain is capable of amazing things, such as writing Nobel-prize-winning psychobiology articles, creating stunningly detailed paintings, or planning and constructing breathtakingly complex buildings like the London Bridge. How does this happen on a biological level? Large networks of neurons coordinate their activity to make this possible. If you think back to the "Key Foundations" section of this book, you may remember that neurons work following an "all-or-nothing" principle: if the postsynaptic neuron gets enough stimulation to go over a certain threshold, an action potential is elicited. The neuron either elicits a full action potential or none at all – there is no half action potential. It was already noted in the 1940s that this "all-or-nothing" principle of neurons bears a striking resemblance to the binary system on which computers are built (McCulloch et al., 1943). In general, the hardware in most computers works on a binary system with an "on" state (1 – the transistor is on and a current flows) and an "off" state (0 – the transistor is off and no current flows). Transistors form the basic building blocks for complex circuits, which can represent and process complex information, such as text, using a 0/1 format within a computer. This is similar to neural networks, which contain some neurons that fire and others that remain inactive, essentially also generating activity patterns based on a binary system. The idea that brain activity can be described in a mathematical model that works in a similar way to computers (McCulloch et al., 1943) was a foundational work for both the field of **computational neuroscience** (e.g., the branch of brain research that uses computer science to understand the brain) and the development of AI.

Due to these parallels, understanding the psychobiology of human intelligence may be highly relevant for AI development. In general, intelligence has a substantial genetic component. For adults, its heritability is 50% or higher, with some studies giving values of up to 80% (Deary et al., 2009). A recent large-scale genome-wide association study (GWAS, see Chapter 9 for details on this method) on educational attainment revealed that 3,952 single-nucleotide polymorphisms (SNPs, see Chapter 9) reached significance (Okbay et al., 2022). Educational attainment is the highest level of education a person has obtained. It is widely used as an approximate estimate of intelligence,

> **Computational neuroscience**: The branch of brain research that uses computer science to understand the brain.

as this data is much easier to obtain than the results of a full intelligence test (which means that many more people can be included, increasing statistical power). Each of the significant SNPs explained only a tiny bit of variance, showing that educational attainment and, by proxy, intelligence are highly polygenic traits (e.g., many different genes play a role in it). Unsurprisingly, many of the identified genes were related to neurons and different types of glial cells, such as astrocytes and oligodendrocytes, suggesting that brain structure plays an important role in intelligence.

Indeed, many different aspects of the brain have been linked to intelligence in psychobiological studies, such as overall brain volume (larger brains are "smarter" across species), but also cortical thickness of specific brain areas or structural parameters of white matter tracts in the brain. An integration of the findings of psychobiological studies on how brain structure underlies intelligence was performed in the highly influential **parieto-frontal integration theory (P-FIT)** (Jung & Haier, 2007). In essence, the P-FIT assumes that there is no single isolated "intelligence brain area", but that intelligent behaviour critically depends on a widely distributed network of grey matter brain regions and the white matter tracts connecting those regions. It includes temporal and occipital regions where auditory and sensory information are first processed. Subsequently, the inferior and superior parietal lobe (the "P" in P-FIT) further process the information from the sensory brain areas and elaboration and abstraction of the information take place. The parietal brain areas are connected to the prefrontal cortex, the most anterior part of the frontal lobe linked with higher-order cognition, executive functioning, and speech (the "F" in P-FIT). Here, active solving of the cognitive task at hand takes place. Afterwards, another frontal area called the anterior cingulate, which is relevant for attention and decision making, ensures that the correct reaction in the environment is performed and other potential reactions are inhibited. In addition to these grey matter areas, the white matter connections between them are also crucial.

Can knowledge about the psychobiology of human intelligence help design better AI, even if AI is based on a computer and not a brain? Indeed, it has been suggested that **neuroscience-inspired AI** (Hassabis et al., 2017) may have several advantages. AI models are often very good at one isolated aspect of what

Parieto-frontal integration theory (P-FIT): A theory that assumes that a parieto-frontal brain network underlies intelligence in humans.

Neuroscience-inspired AI: The idea that insights from psychobiological research may inform the development of more capable AI systems.

the human brain can do (such as some models can play chess better than the best human players, others are really good at generating large quantities of text in a much shorter timeframe than any human could ever do), but are unable to perform any other tasks very well. The human brain, on the other hand, has a wide range of abilities, some of which far exceed what AI can do at the moment, including creativity, dreaming, consciousness, and many other aspects. Also, some motor aspects that seem to be very easy for the human brain, like moving a body on two legs quickly in a highly variable environment with many other moving agents (such as downtown London), are not yet feasible for AI. By transferring insights from how specific brain systems work into AI development, for example, by examining how the brain controls motor behaviour and then implementing similar computational models, such problems may be addressed (Hassabis et al., 2017).

Interestingly, the opposite is also true: ideas and theories from computational neuroscience can also be very helpful in understanding how biological systems work. For example, Marr's framework, a widely influential account of how vision works as an information processing system in the brain, assumed that there are three levels of information processing in the vision system (Marr, 1982):

1 The computational level: the general function of the vision system (seeing things in the environment)
2 The algorithmic level: processing of sensory information from the eyes into representations
3 The hardware implementation level: neural structures in the brain underlying vision, such as the occipital cortex

The terminology used here, such as "hardware" for brain structures, shows how strongly Marr's model is driven by ideas from computer science. Thus, the relationship between psychobiology and computational neuroscience goes both ways, and both of these two branches of science can benefit from each other.

Does using AI too much have a negative impact on human cognition?

In Chapter 4, we discussed how the human brain is a highly plastic organ and that it can change structurally due to environmental influences and learning new skills. Neural plasticity, however, does not always have a positive outcome; it can also lead to maladaptation, brain changes that may be negative for the person. If we do not use a certain skill anymore, the synaptic strengths in the relevant networks get lower, and over time, we get worse at the skill. For example, if someone spends all their childhood practising the piano, they may become a decent piano player. However,

Large language model (LLM): A type of AI model programmed to generate texts.

if they then stop playing as adults, their skills will deteriorate over the years. It has been suggested that relying on AI too much to "offload" complex thinking may have similar unwanted effects on critical thinking ability. This idea was supported by a behavioural experiment that found that people who used AI more showed less critical thinking ability (Gerlich, 2025). Moreover, an electroencephalography (EEG) study on brain functional consequences of writing essays using **large language models (LLMs)**, AI models programmed to generate texts, instead of actually writing them, found that AI use may negatively affect functional brain connectivity (Kosmyna et al., 2025). Participants were divided into three groups: one that had to write an essay using only their brains, a second that could use the help of a search engine, and a third that could use AI. The EEG results showed that the volunteers in the brain-only group had the strongest network connectivity, followed by the search engine group. The AI group showed the weakest functional connectivity. Although these findings are largely preliminary at this point, they highlight the importance of psychobiological research on the impact of AI use on the human brain, particularly in the education system.

Artificial Intelligence as a tool in psychobiology

Have you ever tried writing a poem or song lyrics? Even with a brain as amazing and capable as the human brain, this can be quite a daunting task that can take many hours or even days to get right. These days, poems, song lyrics, or any kind of text can be generated within seconds using the abovementioned LLMs (but, of course, typically in rather low quality). While this type of AI can be helpful for some aspects of psychobiological research (such as help with literature search when planning a project, help with generating code for statistical analyses of data), it is not the main type of AI model used in psychobiological research. Instead, the models used in psychobiological research are typically focused on processing data. A general problem in psychobiology is that datasets are getting bigger and bigger, and it can get quite difficult to conduct analyses "by hand". Imagine a clinical study focused on the genetics of brain structure in patients with a mental health disorder and healthy controls. Some parcellation schemes (e.g., methods to divide the brain into separate regions) for the human brain nowadays include more than 200 distinct brain regions. Comprehensive high-resolution SNP arrays for GWAS can sometimes include data from more than 1 million different SNPs. If one wanted to find out how genetic variation links to diagnoses and whether this association is mediated by brain structure in any specific brain area, 200 million different analyses would need to be performed. AI models can help detect specific data patterns distinguishing brain and genetic markers of patients from controls.

Conclusion

AI can be helpful in analysing psychobiological datasets, but psychobiological research on intelligence can also be helpful in designing more capable AI models. The development of more and more capable AI systems and the question of whether they can (or should) become conscious will be major future questions in psychobiological research and other research areas.

Further reading

Additional academic source: Louwerse, M. M. (2025). *Understanding Artificial Minds through Human Minds. The Psychology of Artificial Intelligence* (1st ed.). Routledge.

Relevant web resource: "AI and the work of psychologists: Practical applications and ethical considerations": An article with recommendations on AI in psychological science on the website of the BPS https://www.bps.org.uk/blog/ai-and-work-psychologists-practical-applications-and-ethical-considerations

Related film: 2001: *A Space Odyssey* (1968). A classic film on the potential dangers of advanced AI.

Related film: *Her* (2013). A movie exploring how a human can fall in love with an AI.

References

Deary, I. J., Johnson, W., & Houlihan, L. M. (2009). Genetic foundations of human intelligence. *Human Genetics, 126*, 215–232. https://doi.org/10.1007/s00439-009-0655-4

Gerlich, M. (2025). AI tools in society: impacts on cognitive offloading and the future of critical thinking. *Societies, 15*, 6. https://doi.org/10.3390/soc15010006

Hassabis, D., Kumaran, D., Summerfield, C., & Botvinick, M. (2017). Neuroscience-inspired artificial intelligence. *Neuron, 95*, 245–258. https://doi.org/10.1016/j.neuron.2017.06.011

Jung, R. E., & Haier, R. J. (2007). The Parieto-Frontal Integration Theory (P-FIT) of intelligence: converging neuroimaging evidence. *The Behavioral and Brain Sciences, 30*, 135–187. https://doi.org/10.1017/S0140525X07001185

Kosmyna, N., Hauptmann, E., Yuan, Y. T., Situ, J., Liao, X., Beresnitzky, A. V., Braunstein, I., & Maes, P. (2025). Your brain on ChatGPT: accumulation of cognitive debt when using an AI assistant for essay writing task. *ArXiv*, abs/2506.08872.

Marr, D. (1982). *Vision. A Computational Investigation into the Human Representation and Processing of Visual Information*. The MIT Press.

McCulloch, W. S., & Pitts, W. (1943). A logical calculus of the ideas immanent in nervous activity. *Bulletin of Mathematical Biophysics, 5*, 115–133. https://doi.org/10.1007/BF02478259

Okbay, A., Wu, Y., Wang, N., Jayashankar, H., Bennett, M., Nehzati, S. M., Sidorenko, J., Kweon, H., Goldman, G., Gjorgjieva, T., Jiang, Y., Hicks, B., Tian, C., Hinds, D. A., Ahlskog, R., Magnusson, P. K. E., Oskarsson, S., Hayward, C., Campbell, A., Porteous, D. J., … Young, A. I. (2022). Polygenic prediction of educational attainment within and between families from genome-wide association analyses in 3 million individuals. *Nature Genetics, 54*, 437–449. https://doi.org/10.1038/s41588-022-01016-z

Index

For Product Safety Concerns and Information please contact our EU representative GPSR@taylorandfrancis.com
Taylor & Francis Verlag GmbH, Kaufingerstraße 24, 80331 München, Germany

www.ingramcontent.com/pod-product-compliance
Lightning Source LLC
LaVergne TN
LVHW020954010926
846999LV00032B/429
9781032933344